THE BIRDING PRO'S
FIELD GUIDES

Birds of Florida

Marc Parnell

Naturalist & Traveler Press

To my mother,
For whom this book was originally intended.

May all readers of this field guide
enjoy birding as much as we have together.

Printed in the United States of America
First Printing, 2021

ISBN: 978-1-954228-03-0
Library of Congress Control Number: 2021932080

Naturalist & Traveler Press
Cleveland, Ohio

www.thebirdingpro.com

TABLE OF CONTENTS

Note: All species listings are alphabetized and located in the rear index for quick reference.

HOW TO USE THIS GUIDE

Birding by Comparison

This field guide series introduces a new method to bird identification: the ***birding by comparison approach***. The objective of this technique is to empower birders to understand how birds might appear in a foreign environment before they have even observed the species, thus allowing them to more quickly and intelligently respond in the field.

First, close your eyes and imagine the size and silhouette of a well-known suburban species, such as the Northern Cardinal. Consider (from memory) how it perches on a branch or birdbath, how large it seems compared to the nearby leaves and vegetation, and how it appears from farther away—such as from across the street.

Now, consider the similarly sized Gray Catbird, a common bird of thickets and wooded edges. While less frequently observed by suburbanites, most nature walks in the warmer months will turn up at least several loudly *mewing* individuals. With eyes closed, superimpose the silhouette of a gray Northern Cardinal into a dense thicket, with the tail visible from one gap in the leaves and the head visible in another. Finally, consider the detailed images and behavior accounts given on the Gray Catbird species page, and modify the mental imagery accordingly.

Such visualization techniques allow the birder to transform each species into a three-dimensional, breathing creature that is practically waiting to jump from the pages. In addition, they prepare the birder in advance for how to locate and identify these birds in a simple, memorable way.

Male Northern Cardinal at left, Adult Gray Catbird at right.
(Note: Both the Gray Catbird and Northern Cardinal are
listed in this guide as measuring 8 ¾ in. from bill to tail.)

Locating Birds in This Guide

When sequentially flipping through the pages of this field guide, you will be viewing all common birds of the region *from largest to smallest*. Once a species in question has been narrowed to a selection of pages, the large images on the left side allow for an easy and painless identification.

In addition, consider the following reference sizes, which may prove helpful when starting out:

- **Very, Very Large**: Great Blue Heron (45 in.), Canada Goose (37 in.), Turkey Vulture (28 in.)
- **Very Large**: Mallard (23 in.), Red-tailed Hawk (22 in.), Ring-billed Gull (19 in.), American Crow (19 in.)
- **Large**: Cooper's Hawk (16 in.), Rock Pigeon/Dove (13 in.), Common Grackle (12 in.)
- **Medium-Large**: Mourning Dove (12 in.), Blue Jay (11 in.), American Robin (10 in.), Northern Cardinal (8 ¾ in.)
- **Medium**: European Starling (8 ¼ in.), Red-winged Blackbird (8 in.), Brown-headed Cowbird (7 ½ in.)
- **Small-Medium**: Downy Woodpecker (6 ¼ in.), Song Sparrow (5 ¾ in.), House Finch (5 ½ in.)
- **Small**: Chipping Sparrow (5 ½ in.), White-breasted Nuthatch (5 ¼ in.), Carolina Wren (5 ¼ in.)
- **Very Small**: American Goldfinch (5 in.), Common Yellowthroat (4 ¾ in.), Ruby-throated Hummingbird (3 ¼ in.)

All species are also listed in the rear index, which provides a complete listing of the birds covered in this field guide.

Understanding Species Listings

Each listing contains detailed information on many aspects of the species' life, sorted into a series of straightforward sections. For more detailed explanations of the written sections, consider the diagrams on the following two pages.

In addition, each species features a full page of color photographs. These have been carefully selected to highlight each species' most significant features and field marks, as well as accurately present the bird in its typical habitat. This should provide a baseline reference when first studying a particular bird, and will thus closely correspond with many field observations.

Frequency Rating: This provides a one to five rating of how likely an average birder is to see the species in a given year. Novices should mostly focus on three- to five-rated birds, while advanced birders will likely be familiar with birds of all ratings.

Common Name: This is the name most often used when describing the species.

Habitat: Describes where the species is most likely to be observed in the wild.

Wild Diet: Describes the food sources most often taken by this species (feeder diet is covered separately in *Bird Feeding Tips*, if applicable).

Migrate: This explains if, or the extent to which, a species migrates in this region.

Eggs: Describes the color, markings, length, and number of eggs. Also, lists the number of broods if greater than one.

Compare to Similar Species: Describes the significant field marks for distinguishing this bird from similar species.

Species Map: Dark-highlighted states indicate the species' presence in the state, while lighter states (of which there are none for the Mourning Dove, a widely common bird) indicate the species' relative absence from the state.

⑤ **MOURNING DOVE.** *Ze*

SIZE: 12 in.
HABITAT: Open woods, fields, suburbs, roa
WILD DIET: Various seeds.
BEHAVIOR: Often observed perching on repeatedly *hooing* with its signature, melanch is not an overly picky eater. To accompany it swallows fine rocks or sands to aid in digesti itself on the ground, with wings and tail spla
MIGRATE? Partially.
NESTING: Hidden among tree branches, objects such as eaves and gutters. Cup-shap grasses, and small sticks. About 8 in. across.
EGGS: White. Length of 1 in. Total of 2. Us raise up to 6.

BIRD FEED

FEEDER DIET: Black-oil and hulled sunflowe hearts, millet, oats, nyjer, milo. **FEEDER TYF**
BEHAVIOR: May rest or forage beneath feede Hawks, and sometimes Sharp-shinned or even R

COMPARE TO SIMILAR SPECIES: M found in less urban areas. Tapered, feathered which are very different from the more recta American Kestrels, not to mention many oth

DID YOU KNOW? Occasionally called turt in flight—reaching speeds of up to 55 mph as

J   F

ʼaida macroura.

Size: Indicates the average length from bill to tail.

ıdsides.

wires, fences, roofs, and in trees, while
ıoly call. Pecks for food on the ground, and
ıs voracious appetite for seeds, this species
ın. Occasionally may be observed sunning
ʼed out.

in shrubs, on the ground, or in artificial
ed, and constructed with conifer needles,

ıally raises 2-3 broods each year, but may

ING TIPS

r seeds, safflower seed, cracked corn, peanut
ʼES: Ground, platforms, hoppers. **FEEDER**
ʼs. Common prey for feeder-raiding Cooper's
ʼed-shouldered Hawks.

ıch paler than Rock Doves, and usually
tails are easily observable when perching,
ıngular tails of Sharp-shinned Hawks and
ʼr visual differences.

ıe doves, these birds are anything but slow
they whistle through the air.

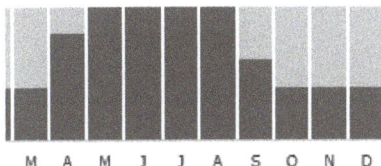

M A M J J A S O N D

Size Category: Provides a convenient, color-coded indicator of bird size. Eight different sizes are used throughout this book, all of which are listed (with examples) on Page 5.

Scientific Name: This is the name most often used in academic literature.

Behavior: This section provides an extended, in-depth description of how the species spends its days (e.g., foraging, flocking, aggression, flying style, songs and calls, etc.).

Nesting: Describes the location, construction, and size of this species' typical nests.

Bird Feeding Tips: For birds that visit feeders, this section describes which types of food are consumed, which feeders are preferred, and a brief description of behavior.

Did You Know: Provides an interesting fun fact for each species, and often much more.

Monthly Birding Forecast: Provides a simplified chart to show when the species is most observable locally. This forecast allows for birders to selectively target certain species by time of year.

INTRODUCTION TO BIRDING AND BIRD FEEDING

BIRDING

Gear Basics

First on any new birder's wish list must be a pair of suitable binoculars. These can be advertised with a dizzying array of specifications and features.

As far as lenses and magnification are concerned, an 8x42 pair is normally best for beginners and intermediates. The first number refers to the magnification (e.g., 8), which should not exceed 10, and is ideally 7 or 8; the second number refers to the size of the objective lens (e.g., 42 mm), with smaller sizes decreasing overall brightness and field of view. If binoculars with too high of magnification are used, the effective field of view is decreased to the point that quickly locating birds can be extremely difficult.

A good pair of binoculars should cost at least $75, but no more than $300. There are many well-reviewed bins that fall squarely within this price range. However, advanced or professional birders may use binoculars which cost up to $2,500. Keep in mind that increases in cost are often accompanied by marginal benefits, and that an inexpensive pair of binoculars can provide nearly all of the same thrills for a lower entry price, especially for novice or occasional birders.

A mobile application with bird sounds is the next logical item for most birders, and several free options are widely available from most app stores.

This field guide does not include written descriptions of bird calls and songs for every species—though many are included—as it can often be difficult to fully appreciate or even understand songs in this format. Consider downloading the free Audubon (by the National Audubon Society) or Merlin (by the Cornell Lab of Ornithology) mobile apps, which provide audio tracks for each species in a given locality. In addition, some apps even identify birds by their calls in real time, but results can be inconsistent and often require prior expertise on the part of the birder.

A few optional extras must also be mentioned. Many cameras, particularly high-zoom bridge models, are now offering optical zooms in excess of 50x for prices less than $300, which likely proves the most logical starting price point. Spotting scopes are land-based, tripod-mounted telescopes specialized for observing wildlife from a distance, and particularly suited for locating distant shorebirds and waterfowl; many of these scopes can offer up to 60x optical zoom, though quality models often begin near $1,000. Finally, for longer hikes, consider purchasing a bottle of high-SPF sunscreen, a high-capacity water bottle, a first-aid kit, and wading boots (for submerged trails).

Approaching and Identifying Birds in the Field

Keep a safe distance from birds, and be wary of making any sudden movements or noises. Many species are extremely wary of humans, and can vanish into a thicket or behind a tree before the birder is even aware of their presence. (It must also be noted that actively interfering with a bird's ability to forage or nest can affect their chances of long-term survival.) Finally, only explore birding patches on public land, and do not trespass on private property without prior permission—even if there might be a life-list bird lurking in the shadows!

When identifying birds in the field, a stepwise process is often very useful, both for remembering information and prioritizing identification steps. Consider the following:

- First, consider the behavior and habitat of the bird. Is it wading in the shallows of a marsh, like a heron, or perching on the shingles of a house, like a dove?
- Estimate the size of the bird relative to that of others you have observed. For instance, is the bird approximately sparrow-sized, cardinal-sized, duck-sized, etc.?
- Determine the color and primary field marks of the bird in question. If the bird is red, medium-sized, and perched in a tree, does it have a crest like a male Northern Cardinal or black wings like a male Scarlet Tanager?
- Continue to observe the bird while considering these criteria, if possible. Viewing a bird from multiple angles, listening to its vocalizations, and observing its general behavior can further elucidate any puzzling identification challenge.

Finally, consider seeking out local Audubon societies or birding clubs. Partnering with a more experienced companion in the field is one of the best ways to double-check observations and learn more specific or situational techniques. In addition, many of these local organizations sponsor conservation and awareness efforts which are critical for the maintenance of nature for future generations.

BIRD FEEDING

Selecting Feeders

The first feeder selected should be a large, squirrel-proof tube or hopper. These are particularly easy to monitor and refill, and can be filled with a high-quality variety mix or with black-oil sunflower seeds.

For a second feeder, consider mounting suet cages on trees throughout the yard. These can be found in standardized sizes, which fit a wide variety of third-party suet cakes. More hands-on birders might also consider applying the suet directly to the tree bark: most suet cakes easily rub onto the trunk, and provide a more accessible food source for many avian visitors.

The majority of feeder setups would also benefit from a large platform, which can be hung from tree branches or fastened atop a tall, metal pole. Platforms best suit ground-feeding birds, as well as many other species which may be too large to comfortably perch at a tube or hopper feeder. The platform is best filled with a variety mix or black-oil sunflower seed offering.

As a bonus feeder, consider spreading excess seed on the ground nearby, for ground-feeding birds (e.g., doves, sparrows) and mammals (e.g., squirrels, chipmunks). This can often be the most cost-effective way to attract the most species to the backyard, though the ground must be occasionally raked to rid the area of built-up droppings or decomposing feed.

After this point, platform cups with dried mealworms, fresh fruit (e.g., oranges, grapes, or apples), or very small amounts of grape jelly can be added, as well as dedicated hummingbird feeders, hanging seed bells, ground-feeding trays, and hanging thistle tubes for finches. Careful experimentation is often a central tenet of successful bird feeding.

Squirrel-Proofing Feeders

Squirrels are immensely resourceful creatures, and are unlikely to turn down an easy meal—particularly at dedicated feeding stations, which present an enticing opportunity. To ensure that bird feeders serve their originally intended purpose (i.e., feeding the birds), consider the following potential solutions:

- Situate each feeder at least 7-8 ft. away from all nearby trees and branches
- Utilize a tall, metal pole, measuring approximately 5 ft. from the ground to the base of the feeder
- Hang feeders from a line laterally fastened to multiple trees (i.e., the clothesline method)

- Set up a dedicated ground-feeding station to divert squirrels' attention, with a platform or section of ground amply stocked with black-oil sunflower seeds and/or peanuts

Try to refrain from using cayenne pepper, or products which incorporate this spice. While partially effective in discouraging squirrels from consuming the feed (birds have far less sensitive taste buds than mammals), this can be dangerous for the squirrels; if the squirrel touches its eyes after feeding, it may attempt to desperately claw out the foreign particles, leading to partial or full blindness.

Situating Feeders

Bird feeders should be at least 8-12 in. apart from one another, providing ample room for birds to access all openings and perches, as well as reducing the stress imposed on birds when feeding in excessively close quarters.

Additionally, it must be noted that hundreds of millions of birds die each year due to window strikes. As such, best practice for situating feeders is as follows: either 25 feet or more from all nearby windows, or immediately next to any windows. The primary concern with feeders situated in the danger zone—about three to 25 feet away from windows—is that birds can generate enough momentum to make a window strike fatal, while not having sufficient time to avoid the obstacle if quickly fleeing the feeder station (e.g., from a predator, or to seek shelter).

In conclusion, situate feeders as close as possible to low shrubs and/or groves of trees: birds feel more safe with lots of nearby shelter. A metal pole can be used to support a large platform, which is often most effective for attracting the widest variety of birds. All remaining feeders should be squirrel-proofed (e.g., weight-sensitive openings, cages with small openings, or thistle mesh tubes), if possible.

Maintaining Feeders

Bird feed must be replaced at least once a week, particularly in hot or rainy weather, when mold and bacteria growth can be most pernicious. In the special case of hummingbird feeders, each feeder should be completely emptied and refilled at least once every five days, and every two days in warmer weather. Otherwise, the sugar water mixture can ferment, producing toxic levels of alcohol.

THE BIRDING PRO TIP

Sugar water for hummingbirds can be made at home with a four-parts water, one-part white sugar recipe. The water must be brought to a boil before adding sugar, thoroughly stirred, and then allowed to cool afterwards.

Each bird feeder should also be taken down at least once each month for cleaning. The following, stepwise process provides a quick guide to this simple process:

- First, empty all seed.
- Second, scrub away any debris or bird droppings.
- Third, soak the feeder in a weak cleaning solution (e.g., one-part bleach to 10-parts warm water), and gently scrub with a towel.
- Finally, once completely dried (to avoid the growth of mold), the feeder can be refilled and rehung.

If feeders are not regularly cleaned, contagious diseases can quickly spread among local flocks. A commonly observed disease, bacterial conjunctivitis, is common in eastern House Finches; first observed in the 1990s, this causes avian pink eye and eventually leads to full blindness, which itself results in starvation or premature predation.

Nest Boxes and Birdbaths

When considering nest boxes, first ensure that the box in question is made of wood, rather than plastic. Furthermore, individual species often require specific sizes and designs of nest boxes. If you seek to target certain birds, consider searching online for blueprints or for well-reviewed nest boxes listed for sale. Many commercially available, decorative birdhouses fail to successfully attract breeding pairs of birds.

On another note, birdbaths tend to be a fantastic way to attract birds to any backyard. Maximum depths of ¾ to 2 ¼ in. are preferable, with shallower areas near the edges of the basin. A central bubbling feature, if present, helps to prevent insects from settling and congregating around the bath.

Birdbaths must be cleaned two to three times each week. Each basin must be completely emptied, scrubbed clean, soaked in a 1:10 bleach-to-water solution, and thoroughly rinsed before being refilled. If these tasks are not completed, the birdbath can become a breeding ground for various avian diseases—defeating the original purpose of supporting local bird life.

Additional Notes

Plant as much *native* vegetation as possible, and consider leaving brush piles for birds—and other animals—to use as a source of shelter. These simple steps can drastically increase both the diversity and concentration of wildlife in the backyard.

Furthermore, if Black Bears are locally common, consider only setting out feeders in winter (i.e., when bears are hibernating). Otherwise, bears can prove to be a very dangerous nuisance: knocking down and destroying feeders, curiously investigating other parts of the backyard, and even approaching the house. Throughout the remainder of the year, use dense plantings of native shrubs and trees, as well as birdbaths and nest boxes, to safely attract avian visitors.

COLLECTED LIST OF FAQs

BEHAVIOR

Q: *Where do birds go to sleep?*

A: First of all, one common misconception must be addressed: birds do not sleep in nests, with the exception of actively incubating females. Instead, birds sleep—or roost—in a variety of other secure locations.

Waterfowl tend to sleep directly on the water, or on protected shorelines (i.e., with plenty of brush, or on islands). Often present in large flocks, ripples on the water's surface can alert the individuals to any approaching threat. Interestingly, standing waterfowl tend to favor a one-legged stance at their roosts, with the other leg tucked into the belly feathers for warmth.

Large wading birds, such as herons and egrets, tend to roost in the shallows or low in trees, depending on the species. Like many species of waterfowl, wading birds are known to frequently sleep on one leg.

Woodpeckers and nuthatches often roost in cavities, such as natural tree hollows or artificial substitutes. Some birds which nest in cavities, such as wrens, chickadees, and bluebirds, may retire to separate cavity roosts as well.

Crows, starlings, and swallows roost communally. It may be quite common for observers to notice several hundred crows or starlings settling in a grove of trees just before dusk, depending on the location. This strength-in-numbers approach increases safety by application of a collective effort to surveil for predators.

Diurnal birds of prey, such as hawks, may sleep on exposed perches (e.g., telephone poles) or tree branches. In colder weather, individuals are more likely to roost closer to the trunks of mature trees, which slowly dissipate daytime warmth throughout the night.

Finally, most other passerines (i.e., perching birds) tend to roost on sheltered perches in densely vegetated trees, bushes, thickets, and brush piles, often depending on their most frequent daytime haunts. If a predator attempts to climb tree trunks in search of a hasty meal, subtle vibrations are transmitted up the tree and warn any roosting birds of the threat. Like other birds, passerines are more likely to roost closer to the tree trunk during colder bouts of weather.

Q: *Do birds mate for life, or do they change mates throughout a single season?*

A: The vast majority of birds form a moderately stable pair bond for the breeding season, though there may be varying degrees of promiscuity (or "cheating"). However, the pair typically separates by the end of the summer, selecting new mates the following spring. Fewer than one-tenth of all birds exhibit non-monogamous behavior over a single breeding season, with the following patterns occasionally being observed: polygyny, wherein the male takes and protects multiple female mates (e.g., Red-winged Blackbirds); polyandry, where each female has multiple male mates (e.g., Spotted Sandpipers); and full promiscuity, where a less discernible, transient relationship between each "pair" is observed (e.g., some hummingbirds).

Q: *How smart are birds, really? And isn't the expression "bird-brain" used for a good reason?*

A: Birds are fantastically intelligent. Many corvids possess advanced problem-solving and communicational abilities surpassing those of even domestic dogs and cats, and numerous other species have been proven to have phenomenal long-term memories and multitasking abilities. Among the smartest families of birds are the parrots and the corvids (e.g., ravens, crows, and jays).

Q: *Why don't birds sing as much in the wintertime?*

A: For many birds, the primary purposes of singing include courtship and territorial defense. However, the breeding season only extends from spring through late summer; additionally, many birds may flock together in winter to cooperatively search for scarce food sources, or even disperse over wider, undefended areas. Consequently, some species may lose the ability to sing during these colder months, while others are simply more judicious with the use of their voices.

Q: *When do birds migrate, and how long does it take?*

A: Most birds migrate north between March and May, and migrate south between late August and early October: with more senior individuals making these trips first. It may take some species up to two months to complete their journeys, while shorter-distance migrants may take less than a month. In addition, many birds (with a few exceptions, such as hawks, which soar on warm-air currents by day) take migration flights by night, touching down in a nearby, suitable habitat upon daybreak—analogous to a hungry, road-tripping family seeking out the first available rest stop with several restaurants on hand.

Q: *Do migrating birds return to the same backyard feeders each spring and summer?*

A: Many migratory birds display a certain degree of fidelity to their previous nesting or breeding sites. When coupled with their prodigious navigational faculties, it is entirely plausible (and in many cases, likely) that the very birds observed a year ago are again present in the same local backyard or park.

Q: *Why is migration season the best time to see a wide variety of species, and what is migratory fallout?*

A: Many species do not breed or winter locally, with this region instead serving as a waypoint during spring and/or fall migration. This means that many birds are only observable during certain, migratory months.

Migratory fallout is an event where a large accumulation of birds is observable in a local habitat, often lasting for a few days after a significant weather event. Birds tend to migrate most successfully in the presence of a moderately strong tailwind, with an extended wind of 10-20 mph often serving as the sweet spot. If a favorable wind encourages an above-average number of birds to migrate, and is suddenly interrupted by a major storm, birds will return to ground as soon as possible. With many migrants most active by night, this may lead to a host of activity the following morning—with birds seemingly dripping from every tree branch in sight.

Q: *How do birds survive harsh, northern winters?*

A: Northern-wintering birds have adapted in a variety of ways to survive cold temperatures. Many individuals puff out their feathers and maintain larger fat reserves in an effort to retain more heat, reduce blood flow to the legs to keep their core temperature stable, engage in flocking behavior by day in an effort to locate resources, and some may even roost communally to survive the most frigid of nights.

Q: *Do birds chew their food?*

A: Birds lack teeth, and therefore do not chew in the most conventional sense. Some seed-cracking birds, such as finches, are able to break apart seeds and nuts and eat them in pieces, while raptors are known for tearing apart a fresh kill with their sharp bills. However, large pieces of food are still swallowed, and must be adequately digested.

The solution for birds is a two-stage stomach: with the *gizzard* serving as a second stomach, behind a conventional stomach somewhat resembling that found in many mammals. In species which consume coarser plant materials (e.g., acorns) or hard-shelled invertebrates (e.g., mussels), the gizzard is thick-walled and holds grit and pebbles (which the bird regularly consumes as part of its diet), with the gizzard crushing the mixture to break down otherwise indigestible materials. If present, any harder materials—such as bone, fur, shells, insect exoskeletons, and seed pits—are coalesced into a collected mass, which is coughed up as a *pellet* at a later time. This latter mechanism is most commonly used by larger birds, such as raptors and gulls.

Q: *How do birds bathe?*

A: Birds like to stay clean, too. In areas with sufficient rainfall, individuals commonly bathe by splashing and briefly dunking their heads in puddles and the shallows of ponds, while species in drier climates may give themselves dust baths. These behaviors likely help with feather maintenance. In addition, birds are known to frequently preen themselves throughout the day, with the bill being used to smooth out the feathers and remove small insects.

CONSERVATION

Q: *What is the state of bird conservation efforts today, and are populations decreasing?*

A: Bird conservation may be as organized today as it ever has been, but many global bird populations are still facing an existential threat to their long-term survival. A widely cited, recent study in *Science* found that a staggering three billion birds have been lost from the North American continent over the past 50 years—an overall decline of about 30%. Major threats to avian populations include outdoor housecats (which collectively kill nearly three billion birds in the U.S. and Canada each *year*), habitat loss and redevelopment, pollution, and the use of pesticides and herbicides.

Q: *Have any North American bird species ever been declared extinct?*

A: Unfortunately, yes. In addition to a number of notable subspecies, there are seven species which have been declared extinct in North America over the past 200 years. These include the following, ordered from least to most recent:

- *Great Auk*, a species of coastal water-bird native to the North Atlantic, which likely reached depths of over 250 ft. while diving and measured over 30 in. Some early reports described this bird as the "Northern Penguin," though it was not technically related to the penguins of the Southern Hemisphere. Last confirmed near Iceland, in 1844.

- *Labrador Duck*, a diving duck of the coastal North Atlantic from northeastern Canada to Maryland, which measured about 20 in. Likely uncommon before European colonization. Last confirmed in New York, in 1878.

- *Passenger Pigeon*, a flocking dove of the eastern U.S., which measured about 16 in. Perhaps the most numerous bird in recorded history, with individual flocks reliably estimated at over two billion individuals apiece, and dense nesting colonies covering up to 100 sq. miles. Last confirmed in Indiana, in 1902.

- *Carolina Parakeet*, the only resident North American species of parrot, which ranged throughout the eastern U.S. as far north as New York, and measured about 13 in. This species was hunted as an agricultural pest, a practice which was highly successful due to the parakeets' tendency to return to the fallen members of their flock—perhaps an instinct honed in an effort to collectively swarm predators. Last confirmed in 1904 in Florida, but additional sightings probable through the late 1930s.

- *Ivory-Billed Woodpecker*, a woodpecker larger than the Pileated, which was native to mature, often flooded forests of the Deep South and Cuba and measured about 20 in. This species has been the subject of intensive searches in recent decades, with several unconfirmed reports from the mature, forested swamplands of Louisiana, Arkansas, and Florida. Last confirmed in Louisiana in 1944, and in montane Cuba in 1987.

- *Eskimo Curlew*, a shorebird of the northern tundra which migrated through the Great Plains, measuring about 12 in. May have been among the most numerous North American shorebirds at one point, but was hunted indiscriminately for meat in the late 1800s. Some unconfirmed reports in the last several decades, but last confirmed in Texas in 1962, or in Nebraska in 1987.

- *Bachman's Warbler*, a yellow and gray warbler which bred in flooded forests of the southeastern U.S., and measured about 4 ¼ in. A habitually early migrant, most individuals are thought to have wintered in Cuba. Last confirmed in Louisiana, in 1988.

Q: *How have changing habitats due to human development affected birds?*

A: With many birds specially adapted for specific ecological niches, the influence of human development has resulted in a set of wide-ranging effects. A few key examples of this are as follows.

Brown-headed Cowbirds, formerly limited to the Great Plains, have been able to move into much of the eastern United States; the fragmentation of wooded habitats for new suburban developments has created vast swaths of fringe habitat perfectly suited for the cowbirds. This species widely practices brood parasitism during the breeding season, wherein the female lays her eggs in a variety of other songbirds' nests, who in turn rear the foreign young. While a natural fixture of its former haunts, this parasitic trait has threatened many species of forest-dwelling sparrows and warblers in its newly acquired ranges.

On the other hand, while much of New England was used for agriculture in the early years of colonization, large tracts of land began to gradually rewild circa 1900 as urban centers began to consolidate around heavy industry. This led to the loss of many grassland and open-habitat species from these areas, such as the Barn Owl and the Bobolink (as well as diminishing populations of the Brown-headed Cowbird), which returned to their former, more westerly ranges—a shift which perfectly illustrates many species' opportunism in embracing new geographies, so long as they match certain habitat criteria.

The practice of replanting forests after they have been logged is laden with additional complications. Many of these replanted forests consist of very few tree species, all of which are fast-growing and planted in such a way to reduce subsequent forest fires. However, birds and other animals require a natural diversity of woodland flora, and many other species specialize in transitional woodland (i.e., rewilding habitat full of thickets and saplings). Fires and seemingly unsightly thickets are, in fact, quite normal—therefore, letting nature take its original course is usually the best practice.

It must also be noted that grassland birds, which predominantly inhabit the Great Plains and Midwest, have suffered far greater declines in the past 100 years than many other types of species. This is largely due to the mass cultivation of arable land for agriculture. Unfettered grasslands have been lost at a historic pace, though this has not been discussed as widely: perhaps due to the subtler visual changes to the landscape.

Q: *What are the effects of global warming on the avian world, and what should be expected in the coming decades?*

A: On average, bird populations have been inching northward in past years, with many species moving approximately 10 to 15 miles north per decade. The multifactorial changes to habitat associated with global warming (e.g., melting permafrost, increased forest fires, drying river beds) are likely to only worsen the issue of declining bird populations in future years.

Q: *What are the effects of pesticides?*

A: Pesticides have been one of the primary causes of the precipitous insect declines of the past several decades. Estimates are wide-ranging, but it presently seems that insect populations have decreased by about 40% in the past 50 years. A startling example of this trend is found in the decline of the once-abundant Monarch Butterfly, with populations of this species having declined by well over three-quarters in the past several decades. Collectively, these events have critical trickle-down effects throughout the ecosystem, and are likely a driving factor behind other animal diversity crises.

Q: *How do large glass surfaces and nighttime lighting affect migrating birds?*

A: Lights tend to attract birds, particularly during nocturnal migration flights. This, in combination with the large glass windows which tend to accompany nighttime lighting in urban areas, has led to masses of stunned and deceased birds falling to the pavement in cities all throughout North America. As many as one billion birds die each year in the U.S. due to window strikes of this nature. To combat this issue, many cities have recently launched campaigns to introduce bird-friendly windows and auto-off lighting in tall office buildings.

IDENTIFICATION

Q: *I saw a fully or partially white bird at my feeders. What are leucism, albinism, and melanism?*

A: Both leucism and albinism can result in the manifestation of unusual whiteness. Leucism results in partial pigmentation, with some feathers developing normally and others becoming a patchy white. This is far more common than albinism, which is a rare condition in which all feathers are white and the eyes are a washed-out pink; this is due to a complete inability to produce pigmentation.

Leucistic female Boat-tailed Grackle pictured above.
Note that a normal individual would be fully brown and black.

Melanism, on the other hand, involves overactive pigment production, wherein the bird has a visibly darker (or even blackish) appearance. This condition is likely rarer than both leucism and albinism.

White-winged Dove exhibiting melanism above. Note that this species is normally a pale taupe (i.e., similar to Mourning Dove), rather than brown as pictured.

In addition, the exceptionally rare case of xanthochroism, or xanthism, results in excessively yellow individuals. This is normally due to a genetic condition, but could theoretically be rooted in dietary causes as well.

Q: *How often do birds molt their feathers?*

A: Most birds molt their flight feathers—or *remiges*—once each year, and molt their body feathers one or two times per year.

Q: *What are breeding and nonbreeding plumages, and for which months does each term apply?*

A: Breeding plumage is often displayed by adults from April until August; this plumage demonstrates the health or virility of potential mates, and may be incorporated into some courtship rituals. Nonbreeding plumage, on the other hand, is usually displayed from August through March. The nonbreeding plumage is normally duller, so as to reduce visibility from potential predators throughout the remainder of the year.

BACKYARDS AND BIRD FEEDERS

Q: *What should I do with an injured bird?*

A: If an injured bird is located, particularly in the backyard, it is normally best to leave it alone for a short period. However, if the individual is alive but remains immobilized, a conscientious birder should locate and contact a local wildlife rehabilitation clinic for further instructions.

Q: *How have bird feeders contributed to the size and distribution of bird populations?*

A: Casually scattering seeds on the ground for birds has been practiced since the first millennium, A.D., but dedicated bird feeders only came on the scene in the early 1900s, with widespread adoption picking up in the middle decades of the 20th Century. Some species which were previously observed at more southerly latitudes, such as the Northern Cardinal and Tufted Titmouse, are common today throughout the Great Lakes and Northeast, while Mourning Doves now stay the winter across both of these regions. Many other populations of native, feeder-visiting species have been bolstered by this rising tide as well. However, feeders are widely blamed for accelerating the spread of the House Finch throughout the eastern U.S., in addition to abetting the localized explosions of invasive House Sparrow populations. In short, feeders have dramatically impacted the avian landscape, but in more good ways than bad.

Q: *Which birds are more likely to push around others at a contested feeder?*

A: In general, larger birds tend to best assert their dominance when visiting crowded feeders. However, woodpeckers tend to frequently displace larger birds, and House Finches often outcompete slightly larger Purple Finches.

Note: For additional information on this subtopic, please see the previous section, entitled "Introduction to Birding and Bird Feeding."

THE
BIRDS

① **AMERICAN WHITE PELICAN.**
Pelecanus erythrorhynchos.

SIZE: 58 in.

HABITAT: Freshwater wetlands, lakes, rivers, and ponds, often in shallows. Nearby islands for group roosting.

WILD DIET: Mostly small to medium-sized fish, also large aquatic invertebrates and amphibians.

BEHAVIOR: Hunts fish by quickly plunging its bill beneath the water; once brought to the surface, the catch is vigorously wrangled from the pelican's large, expansible pouch into and down its throat. An efficient hunter, individuals frequently consume upwards of several pounds of fish daily. May engage in cooperative hunting behaviors with other individuals. Very long, wide wings result in less wing-loading than would be expected for a bird of this size, allowing for soaring, graceful flight. During breeding season, usually roosts in very large groups on islands.

MIGRATE? Yes.

NESTING: Nests colonially with other individuals, often on difficult-to-reach islands. A shallow impression is made in the soil for each nest, with surrounding sticks and grasses also used. About 1 ½ ft. across.

EGGS: Shades of white. Length of 3 ½ in. Total of 2-3.

FEEDER BEHAVIOR: Does not visit feeders.

COMPARE TO SIMILAR SPECIES: Brown Pelican has a much darker body, and lacks a bright orange bill.

DID YOU KNOW? American White Pelicans make frequent stopovers as they migrate through central and western North America to their breeding grounds, which are found near the northern end of its range. While this species traditionally sticks to wetland habitats along the way, it has been known to raid aquaculture ponds for easy meals in a pinch.

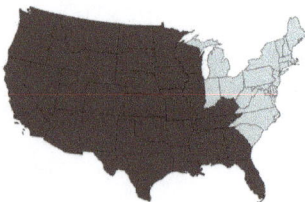

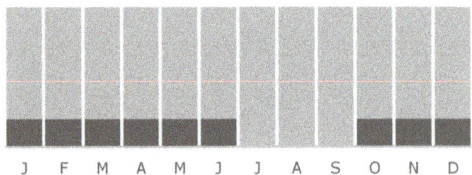

J F M A M J J A S O N D

Adults at top and bottom.

Adult at top (Photo by Paul Asman, Jill Lenoble / CC BY-SA / Cropped,
Adult in flight at bottom (Photo by Net John / CC BY-SA / Cropped).

① **AMERICAN FLAMINGO.** *Phoenicopterus ruber.*

SIZE: 52 in.
HABITAT: Saltwater coastlines and lagoons.
WILD DIET: Aquatic vegetation and small invertebrates.
BEHAVIOR: Repeatedly dips its bill beneath the surface—sometimes while moving the head side to side—and forces water out through small openings in its bill to sift food from the water column. This sifting process is highly efficient, with microscopic openings in the bill preventing all but the smallest organisms from escaping; accordingly, the muscular tongue is highly adapted to facilitating this process, and can pump out water up to several times each second. May move to new feeding territories if foraging conditions are no longer to its liking. Frequently found in large, social flocks all over the Caribbean, and is locally vagrant throughout Florida.
MIGRATE? Not usually.
NESTING: Often nests colonially. A neat mound of dirt with small impression in the center is used for placement of the eggs. About 1-2 ft. wide, and up to 1 ft. tall.
EGGS: White. Length of 3 ½ in. Total of 1.
FEEDER BEHAVIOR: Does not visit feeders.

COMPARE TO SIMILAR SPECIES: Roseate Spoonbill is much smaller, lacks black on wings when in flight, and has a longer, straight bill.

DID YOU KNOW? While archaeological biologists have found that American Flamingos were formerly common in the Everglades and Florida Keys, it appears that most individuals had left by the early 20th Century—likely due to the effects of human encroachment. However, small populations of escapees from Florida zoos, as well as strays from wild flocks, have infrequently visited the Sunshine State in the centuries since, and this graceful bird has consequently become a popular cultural symbol for locals.

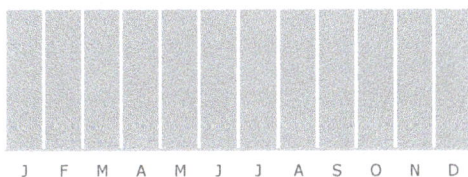

J F M A M J J A S O N D

② **BROWN PELICAN.** *Pelecanus occidentalis*.

SIZE: 48 in.

HABITAT: Saltwater coastlines, estuaries, and islands.

WILD DIET: Small fish.

BEHAVIOR: Often hunts by gliding above the surface of the ocean, looking below for fish. When a target is acquired, the pelican dives into the water, capturing the fish with its bill and pouch. The catch is then brought to the surface, tossed about or manipulated inside the pouch, and swallowed headfirst. Occasionally, when surface fish are prevalent, this species may instead hunt while floating: quickly stabbing the water intermittently with its bill. Usually found in large groups, and may be most visible when resting on nearby jetties, piers, or sandbars.

MIGRATE? No.

NESTING: Often nests colonially. A mound of dirt with a small impression is often lined with sticks and vegetation. May sometimes nest in trees. About 2 ft. across and 6 in. high.

EGGS: Light yellow-brown, sometimes with dirty mottling. Length of 3 in. Total of 2-4.

FEEDER BEHAVIOR: Does not visit feeders.

COMPARE TO SIMILAR SPECIES: American White Pelican has a white body, bright orange bill, and typically frequents freshwater habitats.

DID YOU KNOW? Due to the extensive use of the agricultural pesticide DDT in the mid-1900s, the Brown Pelican began to suffer eggshell deformities and consequently experienced significant population declines throughout much of its range—including a declared state of extinction in Louisiana. However, as DDT was slowly removed from the ecosystem, populations subsequently rebounded; today, with the help of reintroduction efforts, this bird is again common in many coastal ocean habitats.

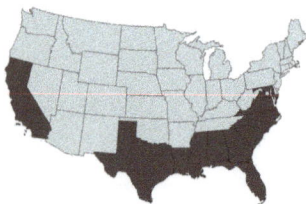

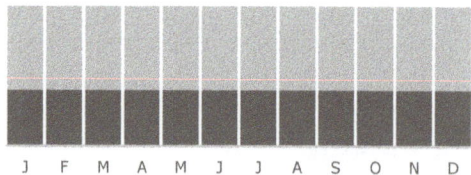

J F M A M J J A S O N D

Adults at top and bottom.

Adults at top and bottom.

④ **GREAT BLUE HERON.** *Ardea herodias.*

SIZE: 45 in.
HABITAT: Coastlines, wetlands, rivers, sometimes fields.
WILD DIET: Primarily fish, though various aquatic wildlife—as well as small mammals and ducklings—may sometimes be taken.
BEHAVIOR: Often observed standing motionless at the edge of bodies of water, waiting for prey. When a nearby fish is spotted, the heron normally strikes from a standing position; however, individuals sometimes chase after their quarry by briskly walking through the water, with head cocked. These birds are usually only seen by suburbanites as they fly from one feeding location to another, though they are among the most common and easily observable wetland birds of this region. Flying motion is languid and wingbeats are somewhat labored, with long legs extended behind.
MIGRATE? Partially.
NESTING: Typically nests in groups (known as heronries) in remote areas, particularly in and atop trees, though some may build nests in safe locations at ground level. Sticks and vegetative debris are used to build a bulky platform. About 2-4 ft. across, and up to 2 ft. thick.
EGGS: Light blue. Length of 2 ½ - 3 in. Total of 3-5.
FEEDER BEHAVIOR: Does not visit feeders.

COMPARE TO SIMILAR SPECIES: Large size and dull blue-to-gray coloration distinguishes this species from other large wading birds. Trailing legs, as well as slow and direct flight motion, differentiate from Turkey Vulture.

DID YOU KNOW? While the Great Blue Heron primarily hunts in the calm shallows, some regional populations have developed their own unique approaches. For instance, individuals on the west coast of North America have been known to stand atop floating kelp beds while hunting, and some in the southeastern U.S. have even adapted to hunt in intertidal zones amid high, rolling waves.

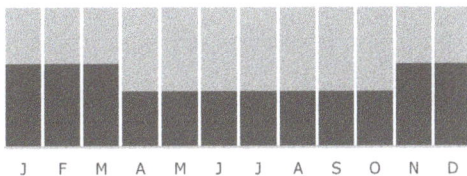

J F M A M J J A S O N D

② **SANDHILL CRANE.** *Antigone canadensis*.

SIZE: 45 in.

HABITAT: Rural wetlands, fields (sometimes agricultural).

WILD DIET: Mostly seeds and grains, but also berries, small animals, and insects.

BEHAVIOR: Forages close to the water surface or ground, normally by the process of combing the substrate with its bill. Often observed in rural agricultural fields, or when flying overhead between roosting and feeding sites—during which the flock gives a series of rattling, bugling calls. Social in flocks, which can number in the thousands during the nonbreeding season at the southern end of its range. Though flocks of cranes may sometimes be vulnerable to various predators, the group is normally wary to such threats; to this effect, aerial predation on the young or injured is often averted by aggressive, airborne kicking motions.

MIGRATE? Partially.

NESTING: Usually nests in standing water, forming a solid mound of vegetative debris. May be reused in future years. About 3 ft. across and 6 in. high.

EGGS: Shades of light brown, with dirty mottling. Length of 2 ½ in. Total of 1-2.

FEEDER BEHAVIOR: Does not visit feeders.

COMPARE TO SIMILAR SPECIES: The rare Whooping Crane is slightly larger, and has a bright white body.

DID YOU KNOW? Sandhill Cranes are well renowned for their mating dances, where the male leaps in the air while flapping its wings, moving its head, and loudly calling. Once a female selects its displaying mate, the pair typically mates for life, returning to the same nest with its flock year after year. This bond may continue for some time, given that North American cranes can attain a lifespan of up to 35 or 40 years.

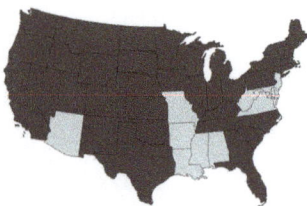

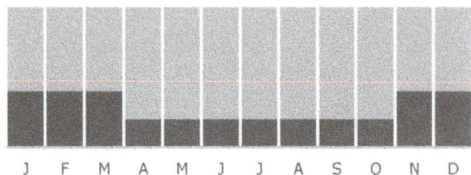

J F M A M J J A S O N D

Adults at top and bottom.

Adult at top (Photo by Mathew Townsend / CC BY-SA / Cropped),
Adult in flight at bottom (Photo by Russ W. / CC BY-SA).

② **WOOD STORK.** *Mycteria americana.*

SIZE: 39 in.
HABITAT: Wetlands.
WILD DIET: Mostly medium-sized fish and aquatic invertebrates, sometimes frogs and insects.
BEHAVIOR: Walks slowly through the shallows with its bill in the water, feeling for prey. Its reflexes allow for nearly instantaneous snapping of the bill when a fish is nearby; even a momentary delay can be costly for a species which often requires over a pound of food daily. Wood Storks soar on thermal updrafts to more effortlessly commute between roosting and feeding locations, often arriving at the foraging site as late as mid-morning. Frequently found in groups, and may nest near egrets and herons. At night, individuals roost in trees.
MIGRATE? Partially.
NESTING: Builds nests in wetland trees, such as mangroves. Sticks are used to construct a platform, sometimes in a tree with many other active stork nests. About 3 ft. across and 6 in. high.
EGGS: White. Length of 2 ½ in. Total of 2-5.
FEEDER BEHAVIOR: Does not visit feeders.

COMPARE TO SIMILAR SPECIES: White Ibis has white underwings apart from wingtips, and lacks a darkly colored head.

DID YOU KNOW? Wood Storks are known for coping with the midday heat by actively defecating on their legs, so as to cool them by evaporation—analogous to humans' tendency to perspire. This behavior is also utilized by various North American vultures, who are the closest relatives of this species. For a time, it was thought that ibises and herons were more closely related, but DNA-DNA hybridization studies were used to help elucidate the matter. This method of genetic cross-comparison seeks to hybridize individual DNA fragments from each of the two subject species in a laboratory setting, and then test the extent to which the hybrid fragments resemble the originals.

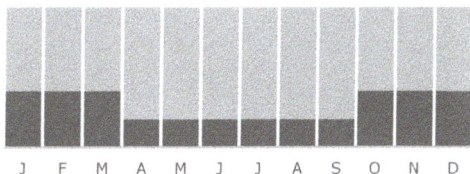

J F M A M J J A S O N D

35

② **WILD TURKEY.** *Meleagris gallopavo.*

SIZE: 39 in.

HABITAT: Edges of woods, especially near clearings and fields.

WILD DIET: Nuts, large seeds, berries, insects and spiders, and occasionally small reptiles and amphibians.

BEHAVIOR: Active foragers, typically walking along the ground. To locate the nuts and seeds which it usually takes for food, individuals often scratch away leaf litter from the forest floor in an effort to uncover any unclaimed morsels. These tidbits are stored along with an assortment of gravelly rocks in the turkey's large gizzard, which slowly grinds the plant matter into more readily digestible pieces. In winter, this portly bird—with males weighing in excess of 15 pounds—may even climb into evergreens to search for any unclaimed food sources.

MIGRATE? No.

NESTING: Areas surrounded by thick shrubbery or tree growth are typically chosen, though some individuals have been known to nest in overgrown fields. An inch-deep depression in the soil is scraped away, upon which the female lays and incubates her eggs. About 12-18 in. across.

EGGS: Light yellow or tan, with red and brown flecks. Length of 2 - 2 ½ in. Total of 8-16.

FEEDER BEHAVIOR: Does not visit feeders, but may be attracted to backyards with native nut-bearing or berry vegetation, particularly if there is nearby woodland.

COMPARE TO SIMILAR SPECIES: Distinctive, and unlike many other birds of this region.

DID YOU KNOW? Wild Turkeys lack adequate night vision, and therefore must roost in trees at night to avoid predators. Individuals have been observed as high as 50 feet above the ground, often selecting some of the highest available perches available in a sturdy, older-growth tree.

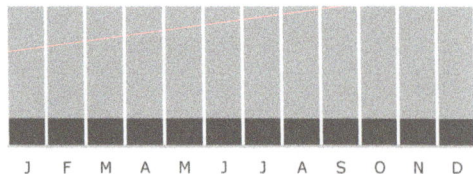

J F M A M J J A S O N D

Male displaying at top (Photo by Vince Pahkala / CC BY-SA / Cropped),
Female with juveniles at bottom (Photo by D. Gordon E. Robertson / CC BY-SA / Cropped).

Adults at top and bottom.

④ **GREAT EGRET.** *Ardea alba*.

SIZE: 38 in.

HABITAT: Usually wetlands, but also calm rivers, lakes, and ponds.

WILD DIET: Mostly small fish and frogs, but also small mammals, insects, birds, and reptiles.

BEHAVIOR: Often observed standing motionless in the shallows of a pond or marsh, waiting to strike a fish that swims its way. This species' feeding technique is similar to that of the Great Blue Heron, with individuals either standing still in wait, or slowly wading into the fringes of schooling fish; this preambulatory stalking culminates with a sudden strike of the bill into the water, after which the fish is swallowed whole in a series of occasionally cumbersome, stepwise motions. Flies with long, lumbering wingbeats as it moves between feeding locations: one must watch for its cocked neck and long, trailing legs. A rattling, croaking call may also be given during these brief aerial excursions.

MIGRATE? Partially.

NESTING: Nests colonially in trees overlooking wetlands, situated dozens of feet off the ground. Platform is constructed of sticks and lined with grasses. About 2-3 ft. across and 8 in. deep.

EGGS: Pale blue or green. Length of 2 ½ in. Total of 3-5.

FEEDER BEHAVIOR: Does not visit feeders.

COMPARE TO SIMILAR SPECIES: Most similar to Snowy Egrets or juvenile Little Blue Herons, but the larger size of the Great Egret is the best and most obvious differentiator.

DID YOU KNOW? While this species does not naturally occur in Europe, it has been known to occasionally wander east of its normal range. In the past decade alone, breeding pairs of Great Egrets have successfully reproduced and potentially begun to establish themselves in the British Isles and in Scandinavia.

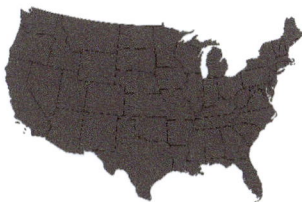

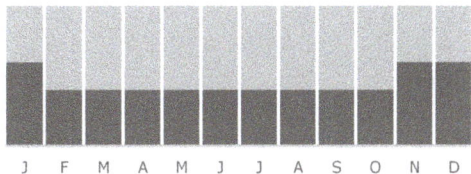

J F M A M J J A S O N D

② **CANADA GOOSE.** *Branta canadensis.*

SIZE: 37 in.

HABITAT: Shallows of ponds and lakes, wetlands, and large fields.

WILD DIET: Various grasses and grains, occasionally insects and small fish.

BEHAVIOR: Often seen in large flocks, particularly flying overhead in V-formation while insouciantly honking. The V-formation is typically employed to decrease wind resistance while affording each individual a forward view; throughout longer flights, the geese will cycle positions to more equally share the workload. Prefers to graze in large fields and lawns, or while floating in aquatic habitat, often near the shallows. This species has adapted very well to human development, with many individuals no longer migrating to the southern U.S. for the winter, as had always been the case before. Consequently, Canada Geese are now commonly observed in the lawns abutting office parks, near urban ponds, or in a variety of other well-populated areas. However, individuals may be aggressive toward humans if they feel threatened, and it is therefore best to always keep a safe distance.

MIGRATE? No.

NESTING: A slightly elevated area is chosen, upon which a shallow, bowl-shaped nest is constructed of loose vegetation and lined with feathers. About 1 ½ - 2 ft. across.

EGGS: Off-white. Length of 3 in. Total of 3-7.

FEEDER BEHAVIOR: Does not visit feeders.

COMPARE TO SIMILAR SPECIES: The far less common Cackling Goose has similar markings, though this species has much shorter necks, stubbier bills, and is closer to 25 in. in length on average.

DID YOU KNOW? Canada Geese are among the most common birds to be struck by aircraft, likely due to their flocking behavior and tendency to feed in large fields. It has been estimated that these birds have caused tens of millions of dollars' worth of damage to aircraft in the United States in the past few decades, though predator decoys and habitat relocation efforts have been moderately effective in recent years.

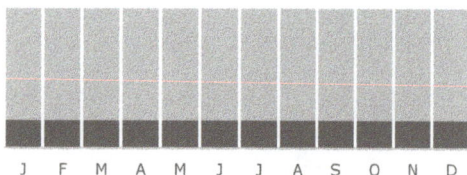

J F M A M J J A S O N D

Adult at top,
Adult with juveniles, or goslings, at bottom.

Adult at top,
Juvenile at bottom (Photo by KetaDesign / CC BY-SA).

② BALD EAGLE. *Haliaeetus leucocephalus.*

SIZE: 34 in.

HABITAT: Coastlines of various bodies of water (e.g., rivers, lakes, reservoirs, and oceans), particularly with adjacent, mature woods.

WILD DIET: Mostly fish (usually up to 24 in. in size), but also carrion, other birds, and mammals.

BEHAVIOR: Flies with powerful wingbeats, often selecting perches in tall, mature trees. Frequently captures fish by swooping low and reaching its talons just beneath the surface, though some individuals may also harass other predators (e.g., ospreys, gulls, and even otters) to steal a fresh catch. The spectacular courtship displays of this bird are among the most widely discussed in the avian world, with male and female locking talons in midair before tumbling downward together—only separating at the final moment to avoid striking the ground.

MIGRATE? Partially.

NESTING: Often selects mature conifers, with optimal location near the top. Sticks and grasses are used to construct a nest, or eyrie, that may grow to be as large as 8 ft. wide and deep, and over a ton in weight. Breeding pairs typically return to the same nests each year.

EGGS: Various shades of white. Length of 3 in. Total of 2-3.

FEEDER BEHAVIOR: Does not visit feeders.

COMPARE TO SIMILAR SPECIES: Juveniles may be confused with large hawks or Golden Eagles. To distinguish, note the mottled, dirty coloration of feathers and the fingered ends of wings. However, the white markings of adults are very much distinct.

DID YOU KNOW? Though Bald Eagles numbered in the hundreds of thousands as recently as the late 1800s, hunting and DDT pesticide use reduced the total number of nesting pairs in the contiguous U.S. to under 500 by the 1950s. Federal protections have since allowed these populations to recover, with nearly 20,000 nesting pairs in the U.S. today. Furthermore, Bald Eagles are now so numerous in the Aleutian Islands that locals of Dutch Harbor, Alaska have taken to calling them "Dutch Harbor pigeons."

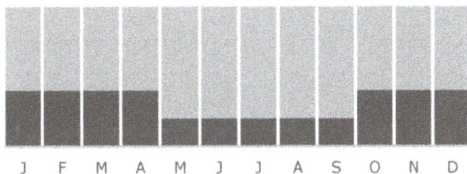

J F M A M J J A S O N D

43

③ **ANHINGA.** *Anhinga anhinga.*

SIZE: 34 in.

HABITAT: Freshwater wetlands.

WILD DIET: Medium-sized fish (e.g., sunfish, catfish, and bass) and reptiles.

BEHAVIOR: When hunting, this species sits low in the water before diving beneath the surface to stalk its quarry. Its long, narrow bill allows for lethal stabbing of prey, often through its side, after which the bird surfaces and quickly swallows the fish. Anhingas are able to actively manage their buoyancy, with individuals slipping beneath the surface and slowly paddling with their webbed feet to stalk prey. Throughout the day, individuals are known to warm and dry themselves with their backs to the sun and their wings spread widely apart. When taking to the air, this species dives from a high perch to generate momentum, or may even run lightly along the surface of the water while strenuously pumping its wings.

MIGRATE? Partially.

NESTING: Colonial nester, often with dozens of its own, or other, species. Messy stick platforms are constructed in trees. About 2 ft. across.

EGGS: White. Length of 2 in. Total of 2-4.

FEEDER BEHAVIOR: Does not visit feeders.

COMPARE TO SIMILAR SPECIES: Superficially similar to cormorants, the Anhinga's wetland habitat is a good differentiator, as is its longer, slimmer neck.

DID YOU KNOW? Unlike many of the waterfowl which share their habitat, the Anhinga lacks waterproof feathers, and therefore tends to sit lower in the water when floating. This also means that individuals must dry their feathers in the sun for long periods of time in between foraging. If they attempt to take off without fully drying, they may experience significant difficulty, or even total failure.

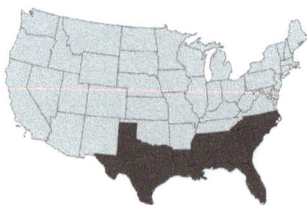

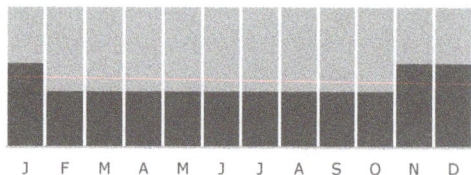

J F M A M J J A S O N D

44

Adult sunning at top,
Juvenile hunting at bottom (Photo by Cláudio Dias Timm / CC BY-SA / Cropped).

Adult swimming at top,
Adult resting at bottom left (Photo by Frank Schulenberg / CC BY-SA / Cropped),
Juvenile at bottom right (Photo by Virginia State Parks / CC BY-SA / Cropped).

④ DOUBLE-CRESTED CORMORANT.
Phalacrocorax auritus.

SIZE: 32 in.

HABITAT: Coastlines, harbors, large lakes and rivers. Infrequently found in smaller lakes, ponds, and wetlands.

WILD DIET: Mostly fish (up to 12 in. in size).

BEHAVIOR: Often observed sitting low in the water before swiftly diving to hunt for prey. This species may swim as deep as 50 feet in search of food. Individuals also form large, conspicuous flocks on piers and sandbars as they dry their feathers in the sun. These flocks collectively consume a great quantity of fish, with each cormorant ingurgitating about one pound of food daily; consequently, cormorant populations in the Great Lakes alone take nearly 80 million pounds of fish yearly.

MIGRATE? Partially.

NESTING: Colonial nesters, usually selecting locations in trees or on protected rocky shorelines. Bowl-shaped, and comprised of twigs and feathers. About 2 ft. in diameter and 8 in. high.

EGGS: Off-white, possibly with shades of pale blue. Length of 2 ½ in. Total of 1-6.

FEEDER BEHAVIOR: Does not visit feeders.

COMPARE TO SIMILAR SPECIES: The adult Great Cormorant is slightly larger and stockier through the body, and has a white flank patch and white patch behind the bill; meanwhile, juvenile Greats have mostly white bellies, and juvenile Double-cresteds only have white on the upper chest. The Neotropic Cormorant is much smaller and also has a proportionately smaller head and bill.

DID YOU KNOW? Double-crested Cormorants are not particularly gracious tenants. After several years of reusing nests in a given tree, the excessive guano buildup on the ground beneath will often kill the tree outright, forcing the nesters to move to another nearby site.

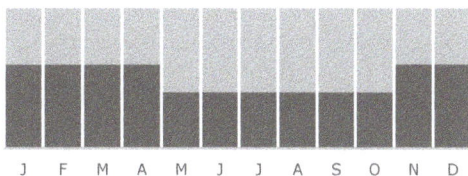

J F M A M J J A S O N D

① **ROSEATE SPOONBILL.** *Platalea ajaja*.

SIZE: 31 in.

HABITAT: Wetlands in close proximity to oceanic coastline. Rarely observed more than 30 to 50 miles inland.

WILD DIET: Small crustaceans, aquatic invertebrates and insects, amphibians, and fish.

BEHAVIOR: Typically wades in shallows or mudflats of less than a half-foot deep, sweeping its bill laterally through the substrate. This motion stirs up benthos, or bottom-dwelling organisms, and lightning-quick reflexes ensure that few potential meals are foregone. Wingbeats are long, slow, and somewhat languorous. Birds are often observed in flocks of varying sizes.

MIGRATE? No.

NESTING: Colonial nesters, usually with ibises, herons, and/or egrets. A sturdy platform bowl of sticks is constructed aboveground in wetland trees and shrubs. About 2 ft. in diameter and 8-12 in. high.

EGGS: Off-white, with red-brown spots. Length of 2 ½ in. Total of 2-4.

FEEDER BEHAVIOR: Does not visit feeders.

COMPARE TO SIMILAR SPECIES: Many a novice birder has shouted, "Look, it's a small flamingo," only to later find out that they had in fact spotted a Roseate Spoonbill. Distinctive bill shape and smaller, squatter profile differentiates from the rare American Flamingo, while pink coloration is otherwise very distinctive.

DID YOU KNOW? The Roseate Spoonbill's dazzling coloration is actually a product of pigments—two, in particular—found in their diet. The reddish pigment *astaxanthin* is responsible for varying shades of pink flight feathers, while the red-orange pigment *canthaxanthin* contributes as well: together making for a truly sensational living canvas.

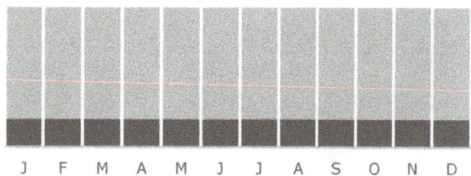

J F M A M J J A S O N D

Adults at top and bottom.

Adults of varying morphs, or colors, at top and bottom.

③ **MUSCOVY DUCK.** *Cairina moschata*.

SIZE: 30 in.

HABITAT: Along urban and suburban lakes, ponds, wetlands, and canals. Also, in fields and parking lots.

WILD DIET: Mostly vegetation, but also insects and spiders, aquatic invertebrates, small fish, and human food waste.

BEHAVIOR: Escapees from captive populations have established growing populations throughout Florida, southern Louisiana, eastern and southern Texas, and elsewhere, often aggressively outcompeting other species for resources and leaving copious amounts of droppings on the ground. While small groups are commonly observed flying between daytime foraging sites and nighttime roosts, individuals mostly walk along the ground while rooting for edible plant matter during the day; however, some also float in shallow water, where insects and larvae are gleaned from the surface. This introduced species' propensity for living in highly populated areas has made their growing presence a somewhat contentious issue in some Florida communities.

MIGRATE? No.

NESTING: Cavity nesters, with an interior lined with grasses. About 2 ft. in depth with an entrance hole up to 12 in. wide.

EGGS: Shades of white. Length of 2 ½ in. Total of 6-16.

FEEDER BEHAVIOR: Does not visit feeders, but uses nest boxes.

COMPARE TO SIMILAR SPECIES: Larger than most other waterfowl, and unique in appearance. Notice the fleshy protrusions on the face and above the bill.

DID YOU KNOW? These ducks are not from Moscow, as the name might have one assume. In fact, the Muscovy is native to the Amazon River basin, and also occurs throughout Central America and the Caribbean. It is likely that the moniker was originally intended to describe a distinct muskiness characteristic to the males.

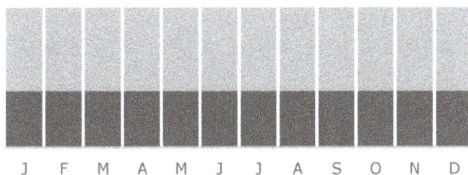

J F M A M J J A S O N D

④ TURKEY VULTURE. *Cathartes aura*.

SIZE: 28 in.

HABITAT: Sparse woods, open fields, roadsides, landfills.

WILD DIET: Carrion, human garbage (up to one-quarter of total dietary intake may consist of artificial materials inadvertently consumed at landfills).

BEHAVIOR: Slowly, wobblingly flies and circles above the countryside, with its long, broad wings held in a shallow V-shape. Throughout the day, this species takes advantage of rising currents of warm air, which enable individuals to effortlessly glide along with very few, if any, wingbeats; these currents, known as *thermals*, are also used by other raptors, such as Red-tailed Hawks, as they scan the countryside for food. Once several 50-degree days occur in a row, Turkey Vultures tend to migrate south for the winter, given that the strength of thermal currents proportionately decreases with daytime temperatures. Solitary individuals or small groups may be observed feeding on carrion along abandoned roadsides.

MIGRATE? Partially.

NESTING: Little to no nest construction. Selects rocky openings, such as caves and crevices, as well as hollowed trees and animal burrows.

EGGS: Milky white with irregular red-brown spotting. Length of 3 in. Total of 2.

FEEDER BEHAVIOR: Does not visit feeders, though can be attracted by animal carcasses.

COMPARE TO SIMILAR SPECIES: The Black Vulture lacks the black-and-tan pattern on the underwing, as well as a red head.

DID YOU KNOW? Turkey Vultures are one of the few birds to possess a sense of smell, by which it finds its food sources. Interestingly, natural gas maintenance employees have repeatedly reported Turkey Vultures congregating en masse after pipelines have burst. This is due to the presence of the natural gas additive ethyl mercaptan, which is also released by decaying flesh.

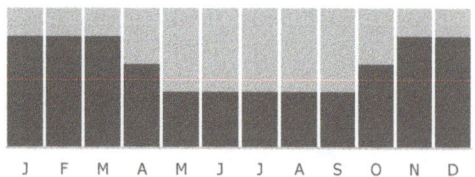

J F M A M J J A S O N D

Adult perching at top (Photo by Devra Cooper / CC BY-SA),
Soaring at bottom.

Adults at top and bottom.

② LIMPKIN. *Aramus guarauna*.

SIZE: 27 in.

HABITAT: Wetlands, flooded forests, and ponds.

WILD DIET: Apple snails.

BEHAVIOR: Forages by wading through the shallows, or by balancing adroitly on beds of water lilies, snagging up to 20 snails per hour with its specially adapted bill. Its bill strength is useful in the process of prying open the snail and incising its tender meat from the shell; interestingly, the jaw muscles flex outward, which allows for maximal opening force. In water with poor visibility, Limpkins may probe bill-down in the substrate, seeking out prey. Additionally, this species can be observed resting on low branches. Occasionally swims between foraging sites.

MIGRATE? No.

NESTING: In a variety of locations immediately near wetlands, and usually well sheltered. The nest takes the form of a roughly arranged, circular mound with inner bowl. About 1 ½ - 2 ft. in diameter.

EGGS: Off-white with variable, dirty staining. Length of 2 ½ in. Total of 5-6, with a second brood.

FEEDER BEHAVIOR: Does not visit feeders.

COMPARE TO SIMILAR SPECIES: Speckling on neck and upper chest, and a less decurved bill, helps to differentiate from juvenile ibises.

DID YOU KNOW? The Limpkin is the only surviving member of the Aramid family, with its companion species having gone extinct long ago. A partial skeleton of a likely ancestor, *Aramus paludigrus* (Latin for "marsh crane"), was unearthed in Colombia in 1998, and was dated to 10-15 million years ago—approximately the same period in which anteaters first appeared in South America.

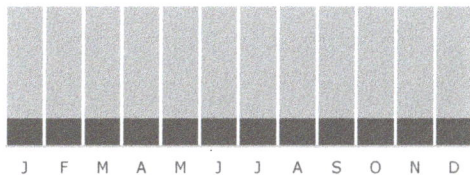

J F M A M J J A S O N D

① **EGYPTIAN GOOSE.** *Alopochen aegyptiaca*.

SIZE: 27 in.

HABITAT: Lakes, ponds, fields, and wetlands.

WILD DIET: Mostly vegetation; also some insects, grains, and human food waste.

BEHAVIOR: Active terrestrial forager, consuming ground-based vegetation as it methodically walks along. In addition, this species is known to consume various forms of aquatic vegetation, with individuals occasionally submerging their head and neck below the surface of the water. Very aggressive and territorial in breeding habitat, attacking other species as well as members of its own: there have even been sporadic reports of individuals attacking manmade objects that venture too close, such as drones. It is likely that this adaptable and aggressive behavior has contributed to the species quickly establishing stable feral populations after escaping from captivity.

MIGRATE? No.

NESTING: Cavity nester, usually in trees. Interior lined with feathers. Entrance hole about 8-12 in. in diameter, interior up to 2-3 ft. deep.

EGGS: Bright white. Length of 2 ½ in. Total of 6-12.

FEEDER BEHAVIOR: Does not visit feeders, but may use nest boxes.

COMPARE TO SIMILAR SPECIES: This non-native bird is very distinctive. In particular, note its prominent dark eye spot and overall tan coloration.

DID YOU KNOW? Just as domesticates of this species are presently found all over the world, it has been hypothesized by Egyptologists that the ancients domesticated these birds as well. Egyptian Geese were featured in many examples of ancient Egyptians' artwork, and were considered to be somewhat sacred. In fact, some Egyptian creation stories feature a primordial mother goose, which laid a single, large egg—with the egg, in turn, spawning the world and all of its diverse contents.

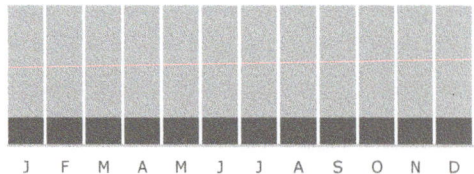

J F M A M J J A S O N D

Adult with three trailing juveniles at top (Note fainter, less defined head coloration on latter),
Adult at bottom.

Adult at top,
Juvenile at bottom.

③ LITTLE BLUE HERON. *Egretta caerulea*.

SIZE: 27 in.

HABITAT: Wetlands.

WILD DIET: Small fish, frogs, aquatic invertebrates, and insects and spiders.

BEHAVIOR: Like many other herons, the Little Blue Heron passively waits for or actively stalks after prey, and strikes when a suitable target draws close. The white coloration of first-year individuals allows them to mix in with flocks of Snowy Egrets, and these juveniles may gain an advantage due to the protection afforded by flocks of larger numbers. A gradual progression of mottling reaches the full, darker adult plumage by the end of the first year, after which point this species is most usually observed hunting alone.

MIGRATE? Partially.

NESTING: Colonial nester, often gathering with other herons, egrets, or ibises. Low sections of trees are selected for nest, which is a dense stick platform. About 1-2 ft. in diameter.

EGGS: Blue-green. Length of 2 in. Total of 2-4.

FEEDER BEHAVIOR: Does not visit feeders.

COMPARE TO SIMILAR SPECIES: Snowy Egrets have bright yellow feet and a yellow spot in front of the eye. Reddish Egrets have a dull red cast to their head, neck, and chest feathers, contrasted with the bluish-purple coloration of the adult Little Blue Heron. Far smaller than Great Blue Heron.

DID YOU KNOW? As is the case with some other herons, this species has a lightly serrated surface along the sides of its middle toes. When raked through its feathers, it removes debris and allows for more effective preening—effectively functioning as a built-in comb.

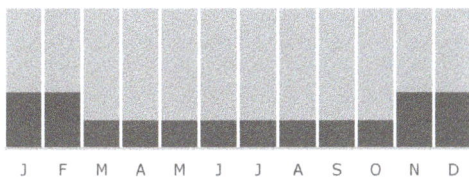

J F M A M J J A S O N D

59

② TRICOLORED HERON. *Egretta tricolor*.

SIZE: 26 in.

HABITAT: Wetlands, coastlines, canals.

WILD DIET: Small fish, frogs, aquatic invertebrates, and insects and spiders.

BEHAVIOR: Like many other herons, this species passively waits for or actively stalks prey, and strikes when a suitable target draws close. Can move quickly and erratically at times when in pursuit, with its wings occasionally extending to maintain overall balance. Also known to attract prey by spreading its wings over the water to create shade for fish, which are quickly dispatched once they take the bait. Adults predominantly rest in the shallows throughout the day, with active hunting behaviors only exhibited for approximately one-quarter of their waking hours.

MIGRATE? No, particularly in southern Florida.

NESTING: Colonial nester, often gathering in trees with other herons, egrets, or ibises. Low to medium heights are selected for nest, which is a dense stick platform. About 1 ½ ft. in diameter.

EGGS: Light green. Length of 2 in. Total of 2-5.

FEEDER BEHAVIOR: Does not visit feeders.

COMPARE TO SIMILAR SPECIES: While Little Blue Herons and Reddish Egrets may seem superficially similar, the white coloration on the belly of this species is distinctive and diagnostic. Even in juveniles, which have a reddish cast to their head and neck feathers, this white coloration remains. In addition, this species is far smaller than the Great Blue Heron, and features a cleaner white belly, as well as burgundy plumage along the chest and throat.

DID YOU KNOW? Tricolored Herons are solitary hunters, and will occasionally act aggressively toward other birds of the same species which venture too close.

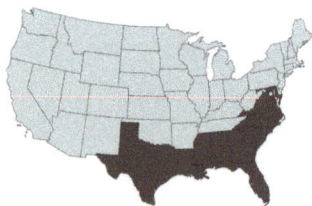

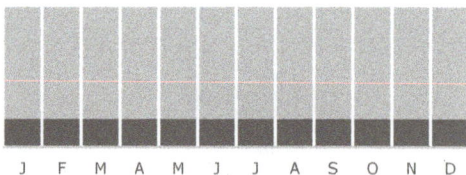

J F M A M J J A S O N D

Adult at top (Photo by Dan Pancamo / CC BY-SA / Cropped),
Adult in flight at bottom (Photo by Andrea Westmoreland / CC BY-SA / Cropped).

Adult perching at top (Photo by Dick Daniels / CC BY-SA),
Adult soaring at bottom.

③ BLACK VULTURE. *Coragyps atratus*.

SIZE: 25 in.
HABITAT: Sparse woods, open fields, roadsides, landfills.
WILD DIET: Carrion.
BEHAVIOR: Alternates between short series of quick, forceful wingbeats and gliding. Often gathers in flocks: sometimes resting on roofs, sometimes flying high in the air. While it does not have the same sense of smell as the Turkey Vulture, it resourcefully compensates by watching the activities of its cousins; if it notices scavenging activity, a flock of Black Vultures will quickly overwhelm a feeding Turkey Vulture and assume control of the feeding site. Only the Crested Caracara of southern Texas readily displaces Black Vulture flocks at carcasses.
MIGRATE? Partially.
NESTING: Cavity nester, selecting locations such as caves, hollows in trees, or spaces in abandoned buildings. Eggs are laid directly on the ground, or floor of cavity.
EGGS: Light tan to light blue-green. Length of 3 in. Total of 2-3.
FEEDER BEHAVIOR: Does not visit feeders, though can be attracted by animal carcasses.

COMPARE TO SIMILAR SPECIES: The more common Turkey Vulture has a black-and-tan pattern on the underwing, a red head, and a visibly longer tail in flight. In addition, if observed closely, the legs of the Black Vulture often extend past the trailing edge of the tail in flight.

DID YOU KNOW? Though New World vultures (such as this species) closely resemble many of the characteristics found in vultures of the Old World, the two groups actually lack a common genetic ancestor. Both lead similar lifestyles, and therefore have adapted convergently: their bald heads are similarly useful in preventing bacterial growth in feathers; pointed, durable beaks allow for efficient tearing of carcasses; and wide wings allow for gliding flights conducive to locating food. Even so, many other behaviors still differ.

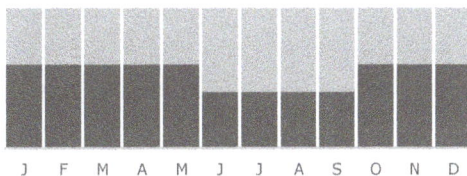

J F M A M J J A S O N D

④ **WHITE IBIS.** *Eudocimus albus.*

SIZE: 25 in.

HABITAT: Shallow wetlands and ponds, also nearby fields.

WILD DIET: Aquatic invertebrates, insects and spiders.

BEHAVIOR: Commonly seen in flocks across a variety of wetland habitats in the American Southeast. May forage in mixed flocks, and moves decisively through the shallows probing in the substrate for prey with its bill. At dawn and dusk, frequently observed flying in V-formation between feeding and roosting sites, the latter of which may host hundreds—or even thousands—of individuals in wetland trees for the evening. In their elaborate, extended courtship rituals, members of this species fly in circles about the females for days before finally settling on a mate. The pairing culminates with the male and female touching heads and wrapping their necks around one another. Individuals may grow somewhat tame in suburban habitats where their feeding patterns bring them closer to humans.

MIGRATE? No.

NESTING: Colonial nester, settling in trees at a low to medium height. A stick platform is arranged for the year's brood. About 1 ft. wide.

EGGS: Pale to bright blue-green. Length of 2 in. Total of 2-4.

FEEDER BEHAVIOR: Does not visit feeders.

COMPARE TO SIMILAR SPECIES: Adult's bright white coloration and red-orange bill and legs are distinctive among wading birds. Juvenile's white belly helps to differentiate from immature Glossy Ibis or adult Limpkin.

DID YOU KNOW? The low height of nests, along with this species' tendency to nest in large groups, makes their eggs and chicks particularly vulnerable to predation. Approximately half of eggs are seized from nests, with typical culprits including the Fish Crow, various grackle species, gulls, and mammals.

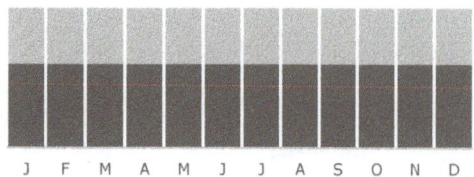

J F M A M J J A S O N D

Adults at top,
Juvenile at bottom (Photo by Dick Daniels / CC BY-SA).

Adults at top and bottom.

③ SNOWY EGRET. *Egretta thula.*

SIZE: 24 in.

HABITAT: Mostly wetlands, but also lakes, ponds, and coastlines.

WILD DIET: Small fish, aquatic invertebrates, amphibians, and insects.

BEHAVIOR: This species often forages and roosts in large groups, including with other species of wading birds. During breeding season, the Snowy Egret engages in spectacular courtship dances: bobbing its head wildly as if imitating a slow woodpecker drilling motion; ruffling its wild, voluminous plumes from the crest of its head to the tips of its wings; flying erratically before diving to the ground and rolling all about; and emitting a nearly ceaseless series of raucous calls. These are very much group affairs, with the females watching attentively and occasionally co-participating.

MIGRATE? Partially.

NESTING: Colonial nesters, in trees near wetland habitat. Platform composed of sticks and vegetative debris. About 1 ft. across, or larger.

EGGS: White to pale green-blue. Length of 1 ½ in. Total of 2-5.

FEEDER BEHAVIOR: Does not visit feeders.

COMPARE TO SIMILAR SPECIES: This species is almost like a miniaturized Great Egret, with notable differences including the Snowy's dark bill and yellow feet. In addition, first-year Little Blue Herons may seem similar, but are slimmer, and lack a fully dark bill, yellow feet, and golden yellow coloration between bill and eyes.

DID YOU KNOW? In the late 1800s and (especially) the early 1900s, numerous egret species—including the Snowy—were hunted for their plumes, typically affixed to hats or headdresses for ceremonial court or women's fashion. The term *aigrette* was coined to describe these ornaments, and many were complemented by a variety of gems and adornments of fine tailoring. However, this practice led to a mass reduction in worldwide egret populations, and conservation practices were set in place to restore numbers closer to their previous levels.

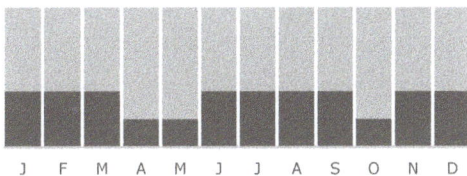

J F M A M J J A S O N D

② **HERRING GULL.** *Larus argentatus.*

SIZE: 24 in.

HABITAT: Coastlines, wetlands, landfills, picnic areas.

WILD DIET: Aquatic invertebrates, fish, worms, carrion, garbage at landfills.

BEHAVIOR: Opportunistic, undiscerning forager at the surface of water, in mudflats and tidal areas, at garbage dumps, and sometimes near urban habitation. Often seen milling around large parking lots, piers, and plowed fields, particularly in mixed flocks of gulls. This gull, like the Ring-billed Gull in particular, has adapted remarkably well to human development. Some individuals have been noted to observe humans for extended periods, with possible benefits including the learning and memorization of various urban threats, as well as the mimicking of human food preferences.

MIGRATE? Yes.

NESTING: A cluster of small craters is scraped away in the dirt or sand, one for each individual egg, and lined with vegetation, garbage, and/or feathers. Often hidden behind an obstruction, such as a bush or large rock.

EGGS: Light green-blue to brown with dark speckles. Length of 3 in. Total of 2-3.

FEEDER BEHAVIOR: Does not visit feeders.

COMPARE TO SIMILAR SPECIES: Most similar to Ring-billed Gull. Note the Herring's pale, pink legs, contrasting with the bright yellow legs of the Ring-billed. Also, the Herring is more stockily built, larger, and adults possess a large, red dot on the lower bill.

DID YOU KNOW? As is the case with most gulls, as well as many other seabirds, the Herring Gull can drink salty seawater without complaint. It possesses specialized salt glands near its eyes, which drain directly through the nostrils and allow for the filtered excess salt to be safely secreted. Remarkably, a single gull has the ability to safely filter up to one-quarter of a pound of saline seawater every two hours.

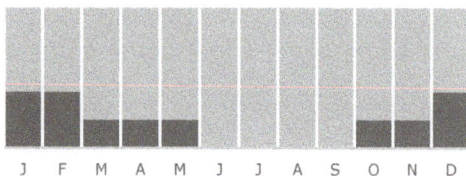

J F M A M J J A S O N D

Adult in breeding plumage at top (Photo by Dick Daniels / CC BY-SA)
(Note: Nonbreeding plumage features dirty gray streaking along the head and neck),
Subadult at bottom.

Male at top,
Female at bottom (Photo by Jamain / CC BY-SA).

② MALLARD. *Anas platyrhynchos.*

SIZE: 23 in.

HABITAT: Wetlands, shallows of lakes and ponds, parks, and fields.

WILD DIET: Seeds, grains, and human-offered food (though offering food is not recommended). Also, aquatic and terrestrial insects, invertebrates.

BEHAVIOR: This species is a dabbling duck, feeding by dipping its head and neck underwater. Like other waterfowl, this species does not possess teeth inside its bill; instead, it periodically swallows pebbles and gravel, which accumulate in the gizzard and help to churn plant matter into more digestible tidbits. Mallards are adaptable foragers, and will often visit fields or parks where human activity has left food scraps, particularly bread crumbs—though these are not healthy for the birds. In parks with a high degree of human contact, these birds will often be quite comfortable around people.

MIGRATE? Partially.

NESTING: Ground nester. Scrapes a small depression in the ground, upon which loose vegetation and eggs are laid. About 9 in. wide and 3 in. deep.

EGGS: White to light blue-green. Length of 2-2 ½ in. Total of 6-13.

FEEDER BEHAVIOR: Does not visit feeders.

COMPARE TO SIMILAR SPECIES: Male is distinctive, but female can be confused with females of other dabbling duck species. American Black Duck females are darker in the body than female Mallards, and also have a dull green tint to the bill.

DID YOU KNOW? Mallards are known for readily breeding with ducks of other species, producing hybrid offspring that can prove an unusual challenge to identify. Species that have hybridized with Mallards include Northern Shovelers (e.g., producing Northern Shoveler x Mallard offspring), Wood Ducks, Northern Pintails, Common Eiders, Green-winged Teals, Gadwalls, and many others.

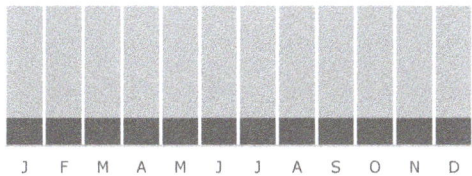

J F M A M J J A S O N D

① SWALLOW-TAILED KITE. *Elanoides forficatus.*

SIZE: 23 in.

HABITAT: Wetlands, flooded forests, and open woods; sometimes forest edges.

WILD DIET: Mostly flying insects (e.g., dragonflies, grasshoppers), but also small reptiles, amphibians, and nestlings.

BEHAVIOR: When foraging, often soars continuously in a series of tight, irregular circles while catching flying insects. Individuals frequently use rising warm air currents, known as thermals, to buoyantly ride along and wheel about in the sky while exerting minimal effort. Adults may also dive for small animals on the ground or take nestlings of medium-sized birds (e.g., American Crow, Mourning Dove), a practice which is primarily undertaken during the breeding season to provide additional sources of protein. This species' long, fin-like tail projections allow for supreme maneuverability in flight, which accommodate its habit of catching flying insects on the wing. To drink water, the Swallow-tailed Kite skims along the surface of wetland water sources with an opened mouth.

MIGRATE? Yes.

NESTING: Selects a treetop location in forested wetlands, often using a loblolly pine. Constructed of woven twigs and sticks, as well as loose vegetation. About 1 ½ ft. wide and 6 in. deep.

EGGS: Off-white with irregular brown markings. Length of 2 in. Total of 1-3.

FEEDER BEHAVIOR: Does not visit feeders.

COMPARE TO SIMILAR SPECIES: Notice the long, forked tail characteristic to this species.

DID YOU KNOW? The Swallow-tailed Kite's wintering grounds reach as far south as northern Argentina, resulting in a lengthy spring migration route through Central and South America—and usually the Caribbean—before finally making landfall near their breeding habitats stateside, which are most highly concentrated in Florida.

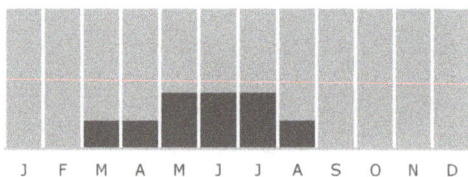

J F M A M J J A S O N D

Adult at top,
Adults at bottom.

Adults with fresh kill at top and bottom.

② OSPREY. *Pandion haliaetus.*

SIZE: 23 in.

HABITAT: Lakes, bays, rivers, and wetlands.

WILD DIET: Fish (less than 18 in. in length).

BEHAVIOR: When hunting, flies as high as 100 feet above areas of shallow water (with wings held in an M-shape), searching for prey below. Once spotted, the individual enters a steep, aerodynamic dive with talons outstretched, piercing the surface of the water upon impact and grasping the fish. This process is repeated with remarkable efficiency; when an osprey is situated in a habitat with sufficient food sources, it frequently seizes a fish in just 10 minutes, and a few dives, of hunting. Often also called seahawks, bayhawks, riverhawks, and fish-hawks, referencing their distinct ecological niche.

MIGRATE? Partially.

NESTING: Selects a high fork of a tree, a clifftop, or a manmade nesting platform. A loose, roughshod platform of sticks. May be reused. About 3-5 ft. wide and up to 3 ft. deep after many years of use and additions.

EGGS: Light yellow-brown with red or brown splotches. Length of 2 ½ in. Total of 1-4.

FEEDER BEHAVIOR: Does not visit feeders.

COMPARE TO SIMILAR SPECIES: Much smaller than the Bald Eagle. If observed in an area with many gulls present, notice the distinct markings of this species; additionally, if carrying prey, the Osprey holds fish in its talons—rather than gulls, which hold prey with their bills.

DID YOU KNOW? Ospreys are one of the only raptor species in the world with a reversible outer toe, which allows for this species to have two toes on both the front and back when gripping slimy, wet fish prey. They also possess small, barb-like grips on the pads of their feet, which allow for an even more secure hold.

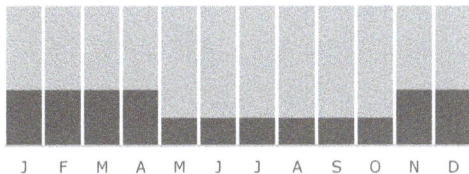

J F M A M J J A S O N D

75

② **GLOSSY IBIS.** *Plegadis falcinellus.*

SIZE: 23 in.

HABITAT: Shallow wetlands, ponds, and streams; fields.

WILD DIET: Aquatic invertebrates, insects and spiders, reptiles, amphibians, fish, and occasionally grains.

BEHAVIOR: Like the White Ibis, this species frequently flocks when foraging, roosting, and anytime in between. Individuals carefully probe throughout the bottom of the water column, stirring up organic matter and quickly nabbing any potential prey items. This activity may bring flocking waders, such as Snowy Egrets, to investigate. Flocks will often fly in V-formation between feeding and roosting sites, the latter of which can draw hundreds of birds to perch in the subcanopies of wetland swamps and mangrove stands.

MIGRATE? Partially.

NESTING: Colonial nester, nesting in trees at a low to medium height. A messy stick platform is arranged for the year's brood. About 1 ft. wide.

EGGS: Pale to bright blue-green. Length of 2 in. Total of 2-5.

FEEDER BEHAVIOR: Does not visit feeders.

COMPARE TO SIMILAR SPECIES: Adult's dark coloration and trademark sickle-shaped bill distinguish from most other wading birds. White-faced Ibis has red coloration between the bill and eye, rather than the dark coloration observable in the Glossy—both of which are clearly outlined in white.

DID YOU KNOW? Glossy Ibises tend to wander more than other species from their established natural range, particularly if current locations are not providing sufficient amounts of food. This has led to a colonization pattern over the past century that has stretched up much of the Atlantic coast, regularly treating Northern birders to the bright colors often reserved for neotropical avifauna.

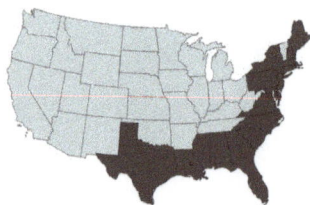

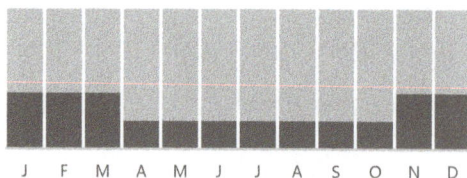

J F M A M J J A S O N D

Adult at top (Photo by Charles J. Sharp / CC BY-SA / Cropped),
Juvenile at bottom.

Male at top,
Female at bottom.

① RED-BREASTED MERGANSER.
Mergus serrator.

SIZE: 22 in.

HABITAT: Coastlines of oceans, large lakes (e.g., Great Lakes), and large rivers.

WILD DIET: Mostly small fish, but also aquatic invertebrates and amphibians.

BEHAVIOR: A diving duck, this species dives with a soft, deft jump from its floating position into the depths below. It usually hunts minnow-sized fish, consuming up to two dozen each day. Group hunting tactics are sometimes used, wherein a group of schooling fish is herded into shallower waters by an arc-shaped formation of mergansers.

MIGRATE? Yes.

NESTING: Nests on the ground in a well-sheltered location, sometimes near a fallen tree. A shallow depression is formed, upon which loose vegetation and feathers are placed. About 1 ft. across.

EGGS: Off-white. Length of 2 ½ in. Total of 4-16.

FEEDER BEHAVIOR: Does not visit feeders.

COMPARE TO SIMILAR SPECIES: Common Merganser also has males with green heads and females with red heads, with a similar silhouette. However, male Common Mergansers have a white body (apart from upper back) and lack a reddish breast; meanwhile, male Red-breasteds have brown and white sides, a trailing tuft on the head, and a white stripe on the neck *with a red-brown upper chest*. In addition, female Red-breasteds have paler head and neck coloration than their Common counterparts.

DID YOU KNOW? Among the merganser species, the Red-breasted has the greatest affinity for larger bodies of water, including oceans and the Great Lakes.

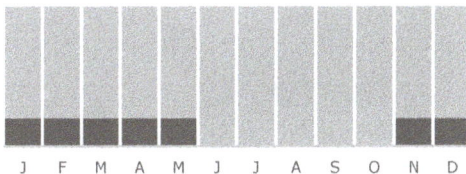

J   F   M   A   M   J   J   A   S   O   N   D

79

① **RED-TAILED HAWK.** *Buteo jamaicensis.*

SIZE: 22 in.
HABITAT: Nearly anywhere, but prefers open woods, fields, and roadsides.
WILD DIET: Mostly small mammals (in particular, squirrels). Less frequently, birds, reptiles, and carrion.
BEHAVIOR: Often observed soaring or circling gracefully in the sky, with light wingbeats, though individuals also perch in trees or on telephone poles. While driving along a highway or interstate, this species is commonly present in perches along the roadside—much more visible in winter, after most leaves have fallen. The Red-tailed Hawk, like many raptors, possesses phenomenal visual acuity; a lone squirrel darting through brush and long grass can be spotted from up to 300 feet away. Once its quarry has been sighted, the hawk swoops low with strong wingbeats, culminating with a forceful strike of the talons, which may stun the prey. Upon its secure capture, the hawk normally carries its prey to a safe perch for consumption. Its familiar, piercing call is often heard in the background of Western-genre films, and is usually given in flight.
MIGRATE? Partially.
NESTING: Typically situated atop a large tree or similarly habitable human-made structure (e.g., billboards). Piles of sticks up to 3 ft. across, and up to 5 ft. deep.
EGGS: White, with some brown blotching. Length of 2 ½ in. Total of 2-5.
FEEDER BEHAVIOR: Uncommonly hunts near feeders.

COMPARE TO SIMILAR SPECIES: Similar to Red-shouldered Hawk in shape, but note pale undersides, dark band of streaking across upper belly, and light red coloration on underside of tail.

DID YOU KNOW? The ancient practice of falconry, whereby humans train captive raptors to hunt animals on their behalf, is continued today by nearly 5,000 Americans— who must first secure a regulatory permit and a registered sponsor. The Red-tailed Hawk, along with the Red-shouldered Hawk, is one of only two North American hawks approved for use by trainees or apprentices; consequently, the Red-tailed is also the most common raptor used by North American falconers, with some hawks adapting to trained hunting techniques in a mere two weeks.

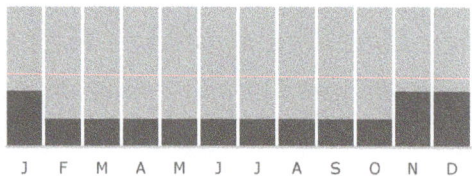

J F M A M J J A S O N D

Perching adult at top,
Soaring adult at bottom (Photo by Tom Koerner / CC BY-SA).

Perching adult at top (Photo by James E. Smallwood / CC BY-SA),
Soaring juvenile at bottom (Photo by Bettina Arrigoni / CC BY-SA / Cropped).

③ RED-SHOULDERED HAWK. *Buteo lineatus.*

SIZE: 21 in.

HABITAT: Open woods, flooded woods.

WILD DIET: Mostly small mammals (such as mice and chipmunks), as well as birds, reptiles, and fish.

BEHAVIOR: The Red-shouldered Hawk tends to hunt more frequently from a perch than its Red-tailed counterpart, but individuals may also be occasionally observed circling and soaring in the open skies. When hunting, the Red-shouldered often finds a semi-concealed perch in a grove of trees, monitoring the gaps in the forest floor for any ground-dwellers brave enough to reveal themselves. After a low, powerful swoop and a downward strike of the talons, the hawk secures its catch and consumes from a nearby perch.

MIGRATE? No.

NESTING: Typically situated in the fork of a deciduous tree, near but not at the top. Piles of sticks up to 2 ft. across and 3 ft. deep, depending on the geometry of the fork.

EGGS: White with some brown blotching. Length of 2 in. Total of 3-5.

FEEDER BEHAVIOR: Uncommonly hunts near feeders.

COMPARE TO SIMILAR SPECIES: Similar to Red-tailed Hawk in shape, but note the red present on the upper chest (present in adults) and the black-and-white striped pattern on the underside of its tail (present in both adults and juveniles).

DID YOU KNOW? As recently as the early 1900s, this species was among the most common of all North American raptors. However, the deforestation and clearing of mature woodland across the U.S. has led to a significant drop in Red-shouldered Hawk numbers, which has correlated with a rise in Red-tailed Hawk numbers. This shift is directly attributable to the habitats preferred by each species, with Red-taileds typically found in more open country and Red-shouldereds in wooded areas.

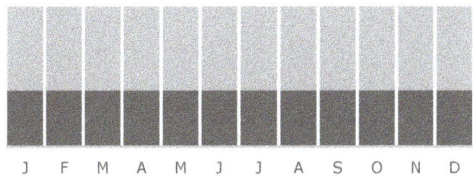

J   F   M   A   M   J   J   A   S   O   N   D

③ **MOTTLED DUCK.** *Anas fulvigula.*

SIZE: 21 in.

HABITAT: Inland wetlands, usually no more than 150 mi. from the oceanic coast.

WILD DIET: Mostly aquatic vegetation, but also aquatic invertebrates and even small fish.

BEHAVIOR: Forages primarily by dabbling, or upending itself, in the shallow waters of wetlands, often reaching to the bottom to pull vegetation from its roots. May also be observed in flooded grain fields, where they employ similar foraging methods. Often crossbreeds with the closely related Mallard, resulting in so-called "muddled ducks," with the males' washed-out green heads and variable body plumage easily confounding the novice birder.

MIGRATE? No.

NESTING: Within a quarter-mile of a nearby lake, river, or pond; a small impression is carved in the soil near semi-dense shrub cover. Loose vegetation and feathers are used to line the interior. About 8 in. across.

EGGS: Milky white. Length of 2 ½ in. Total of 6-12.

FEEDER BEHAVIOR: Does not visit feeders.

COMPARE TO SIMILAR SPECIES: Similar to American Black Ducks, but paler coloration across the entirety of the body, and more richly patterned body feathers. Most distinctive characteristic is the large black spot at the tip of its yellow bill, which is not shared by any other duck species in this region.

DID YOU KNOW? As with the Mexican Duck of the American Southwest, this species is threatened by the ever-growing populations of the Mallard, which is known to readily crossbreed with the Mottled. As populations become more "muddled," particularly in Florida, there is a danger that the Mottled's species-specific gene pool will be eventually lost to that of the Mallard—much like a drop of ketchup irretrievably mixed into a bowl of barbecue sauce.

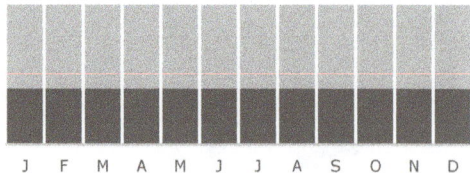

J F M A M J J A S O N D

Adults at top (Photo by Dick Daniels / CC BY-SA / Cropped),
Close-up of adult at bottom (Photo by Judy Gallagher / CC BY-SA / Cropped).

Breeding male at top,
Female with ducklings at bottom.

② **WOOD DUCK.** *Aix sponsa.*

SIZE: 20 in.

HABITAT: Wetlands and small waterways.

WILD DIET: Nuts, seeds, and berries; also, some aquatic invertebrates and insects.

BEHAVIOR: Forages by dabbling in the shallows or by slowly, adroitly walking on land. Tends to prefer sheltered habitats that offer plenty of shelter from predators, such as large raptors. Like other dabbling ducks which ply their trade in secluded wetlands, this species is flushed easily by human activity.

MIGRATE? Partially.

NESTING: Cavity nester. Natural hollows of mature trees (near water) are usually selected, often dozens of feet off the ground. The entry hole may be as small as 4-6 in. in diameter, but this species can adapt to a variety of cavity sizes. Lined with ample feathers.

EGGS: White to off-white. Length of 2 in. Total of 7-17, with 1-2 broods.

FEEDER BEHAVIOR: Does not visit feeders, but uses nest boxes.

COMPARE TO SIMILAR SPECIES: Male is very distinctive in breeding plumage. Nonbreeding and eclipse (molting, occurs during summer) males have washed-out coloration, and usually no green on head. Meanwhile, females have a noticeable white eye patch which extends toward the back of the head.

DID YOU KNOW? As with other duck species, male Wood Ducks are known as drakes, and females as hens. All ducks undergo full molts of their flight feathers during the warmer months, which render them completely flightless for several weeks. In order to better avoid predation and other perceived threats, dabbling ducks such as the Wood Duck tend to situate themselves in the densely vegetated corners of marshes for this period, which provide ample cover. Accordingly, the more brightly colored drakes display a washed-out eclipse plumage during this time to provide better concealment.

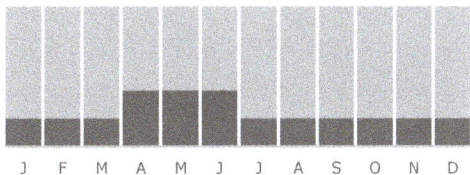

J F M A M J J A S O N D

② **CATTLE EGRET.** *Bubulcus ibis.*

SIZE: 20 in.

HABITAT: Fields and farmland (often with livestock), wetlands.

WILD DIET: Mostly insects and spiders.

BEHAVIOR: Often accompanies slow-moving livestock in agricultural pastures, feeding on the insects temporarily displaced by the farm animals' feeding activity. It may even perch on top of cattle as it waits to embark on its next foraging spree. In a similar vein, individuals may also opportunistically seek out recently plowed fields. This species flocks in very large groups when breeding and roosting, though it may forage either solitarily or with others.

MIGRATE? No.

NESTING: Colonial nester. Usually selects various branches of trees in a wetland habitat, near densely established egret or heron colonies. Piles of sticks form a loose bowl shape. About 1 ½ ft. across and 8 in. deep.

EGGS: Pale blue. Length of 1 ½ - 2 in. Total of 2-4.

FEEDER BEHAVIOR: Does not visit feeders.

COMPARE TO SIMILAR SPECIES: Similar to Snowy Egret, but smaller with shorter neck, yellow bill, and dark-colored (rather than bright yellow) feet.

DID YOU KNOW? The Cattle Egret was originally native to Africa and the southwestern Mediterranean, but vagrants were spotted in the late 1800s in northeastern South America, and became established by the 1930s. Over the course of the following half-century, this species colonized most of South and Central America, as well as the United States—continuing to gradually expand its range northward to this day. It is thought that this is partly due to the recent proliferation of suitable habitat, namely farmland and agricultural pasture.

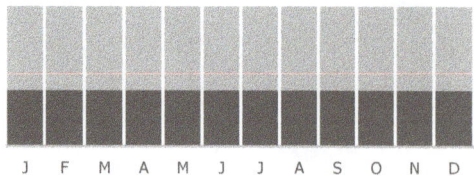

J F M A M J J A S O N D

Adult at top,
Adult with livestock at bottom.

Male at top,
Female and male at bottom.

① **AMERICAN WIGEON.** *Mareca americana.*

SIZE: 20 in.
HABITAT: Wetlands, lakes, and ponds. Also, suburban fields and lawns.
WILD DIET: Mostly vegetation, both aquatic and terrestrial.
BEHAVIOR: A dabbling duck, this species forages by upending itself in the water, with its tail pointed nearly straight up to the sky. Its diet—which is among the most strictly vegetarian of all dabbling ducks—also consists of grasses grazed from fields, lawns, and grasslands. The American Wigeon's stubby, almost goose-like bill is uniquely adapted to this form of terrestrial grazing, though it also provides ample leverage when harvesting submerged, underwater grasses. Flocks begin to migrate south as the leaves turn color, as they require a stable source of green foodstuffs year round. Individuals may also loosely associate with foraging flocks of American Coots.
MIGRATE? Yes.
NESTING: Selects a location in grasslands, somewhat near water. A small impression is excavated, after which the nest is lined with twigs and grasses. About 6-9 in. across.
EGGS: Milky white. Length of 2 in. Total of 5-12.
FEEDER BEHAVIOR: Does not visit feeders.

COMPARE TO SIMILAR SPECIES: Male has a distinctive green patch of coloration from its eye to the back of its head, and also features a white head crown. Females have the stubby bill of the male, in addition to a dark patch around the eye.

DID YOU KNOW? This species is a close cousin of the Eurasian Wigeon, which—though native to Europe, Asia, and North Africa—has been known to appear as a somewhat uncommon vagrant throughout the United States and southern Canada. Eurasian males have a chestnut colored head with a whitish-tan patch on the crest, while females often have a more reddish-brown head.

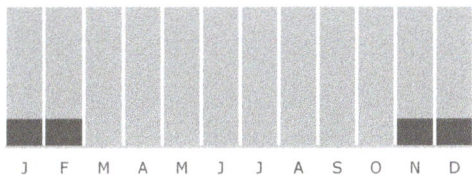

J F M A M J J A S O N D

② BLACK-BELLIED WHISTLING-DUCK.
Dendrocygna autumnalis.

SIZE: 20 in.

HABITAT: Wetlands, sometimes fields and thickets.

WILD DIET: Aquatic and terrestrial vegetation, agricultural grains. Sometimes insects and spiders.

BEHAVIOR: This long-legged duck is well-accustomed to walking on land or lounging in thickets or trees—sometimes even on high stumps, fence posts, or electrical wires. Individuals usually forage at night by dabbling in shallow wetlands or by nibbling on vegetation, seeds, or grains in (sometimes agricultural) fields. Due to this nocturnal activity, this species is one of the ducks that is most susceptible to owl attacks. Known to regularly wander northward as a vagrant, as far as southeastern Canada.

MIGRATE? Partially.

NESTING: Cavity nester. Typically uses natural tree hollows, in which some feathers may be placed to insulate the eggs. Opening is typically 6 in. or larger. May lay eggs in the nests of other whistling-duck mothers, with some nests consequently hosting many dozens of young.

EGGS: Shades of white. Length of 2 in. Total of 9-17, with 1-2 broods.

FEEDER BEHAVIOR: Not expected to visit feeders, but does use nest boxes.

COMPARE TO SIMILAR SPECIES: Black coloration on lower belly, bright red-pink legs and bill, rich brown chest, and light-gray coloration on side of head all distinguish from the Fulvous Whistling-Duck.

DID YOU KNOW? The "whistling-duck" name comes from this species' (and its relatives') tendency to emit a squeaky whistling sound during a variety of activities, such as when flying, roosting, or foraging. However, its unusual tendency—at least, for a duck—to perch in trees lent it the familiar moniker "tree-duck" in the past as well.

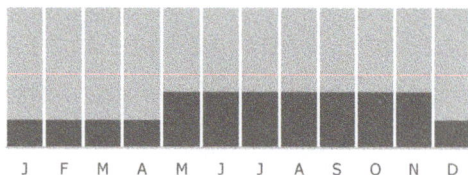

J F M A M J J A S O N D

Adults resting at top,
Adults flying at bottom.

Adult in breeding plumage at top (Photo by Mdf / CC BY-SA / Cropped),
Adult in nonbreeding plumage at bottom (Notice light, dirty streaking on head and neck).

③ RING-BILLED GULL. *Larus delawarensis.*

SIZE: 19 in.

HABITAT: Coastlines, wetlands, landfills, picnic areas.

WILD DIET: Insects, fish, worms, grains, rodents, garbage at landfills.

BEHAVIOR: Forages at the surface of water, in mudflats and tidal areas, at garbage dumps, and sometimes near urban habitation. Often seen milling about or orderly standing in large parking lots and on piers. Individuals tend to exhibit an uncanny degree of resourcefulness, with a highly varied diet and a well-adapted lifestyle to the modern Anthropocene. Individuals may regularly visit the dumpsters near picnic areas or fast-food restaurants, seeking out food scraps and even the small flying insects which gather overhead. In areas with higher degrees of human contact, Ring-billed Gulls have been known to approach humans for food, even nabbing unguarded morsels from outdoor benches and tables.

MIGRATE? Yes.

NESTING: Nests in groups of up to many thousands on sand, concrete, and rocky beaches. Little to no nest lining.

EGGS: Light blue-green to light brown, with dark splotching. Length of 2 ½ in. Total of 3.

FEEDER BEHAVIOR: Does not visit feeders.

COMPARE TO SIMILAR SPECIES: Most similar to Herring Gull. Note the Ring-billed's bright, yellow legs, contrasted with the pale, pink legs of the Herring Gull. Ring-billed Gulls are also smaller, more slight of build, and are most likely to have a sharply defined black ring near the end of the bill.

DID YOU KNOW? Ring-billed Gulls are able to accurately sense their magnetic bearings as soon as they are a few days old. This navigational aptitude allows them to accurately judge the correct direction for their migration routes.

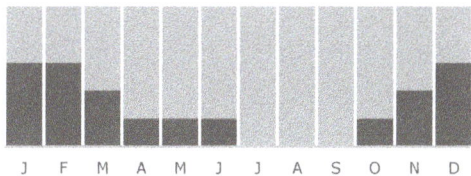

J F M A M J J A S O N D

① **NORTHERN SHOVELER.** *Spatula clypeata.*

SIZE: 19 in.

HABITAT: Mostly wetlands, also lakes and ponds during fall and winter.

WILD DIET: Aquatic invertebrates and algae. Uncommonly, aquatic vegetation.

BEHAVIOR: A dabbling duck, this species forages by upending itself in the shallows as it forages for prey. More commonly, individuals also swim with their bills skimming, sweeping, or partially submerged beneath the water surface. The notched edges of its inner bill act like a sieve, allowing for invertebrates—including organisms as small as plankton—to be efficiently filtered from the water. Consequently, this duck is adaptable to varying qualities of wetland habitat, allowing individuals to forage in wetland areas which might not have sufficient nutrients for other dabbling ducks. Shovelers may flock in small groups, but are less likely to do so than many other dabbling ducks. Occasionally, this species may be observed walking or roosting on land.

MIGRATE? Yes.

NESTING: Selects a grassy site near wetlands. A bowl is scraped into the ground and lined with twigs, vegetation, and feathers. Up to 1 ft. across.

EGGS: White to off-white. Length of 2 in. Total of 8-11.

FEEDER BEHAVIOR: Does not visit feeders.

COMPARE TO SIMILAR SPECIES: Best distinguished by the long, wide, and shovel-like bill present in all individuals of this species, though the female's drab coloration may initially resemble that of other waterfowl.

DID YOU KNOW? When incubating females of this species are threatened by nest predators, they quickly defecate on the eggs before fleeing. This may serve one of two purposes: concealing the appearance and smell of the eggs, or deterring the predator from consuming a potentially disease-ridden meal.

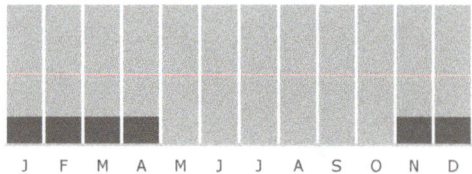

J F M A M J J A S O N D

Breeding male at top,
Nonbreeding males at center,
Female at bottom.

Adults at top and bottom.

① FULVOUS WHISTLING-DUCK.
Dendrocygna bicolor.

SIZE: 19 in.

HABITAT: Wetlands, also agricultural fields.

WILD DIET: Aquatic and terrestrial vegetation, agricultural grains. Sometimes insects and spiders.

BEHAVIOR: This whistling-duck is characterized by its long, blue-gray legs and bill, as well as its gregarious feeding practices: frequently in flooded agricultural fields, such as rice paddies. When feeding in shallow wetlands, may either dabble in the shallows or occasionally dive for vegetation just out of neck's reach. Often filter feeds by forcing water through small openings in its bill. May forage by day or by night, and often shares roosting or feeding locations with other species of whistling-duck, making thorough identification practices all the more important.

MIGRATE? No.

NESTING: Selects a location in a flooded agricultural field or shallow wetland, in water or on dry land. Grasses and stems are woven into a somewhat tidy bowl, about 15 in. across. Often lays its eggs in nests of other whistling-ducks, sometimes resulting in very large combined clutch sizes.

EGGS: White. Length of 2 in. Total of 8-13, with 1-2 broods.

FEEDER BEHAVIOR: Not expected to visit feeders.

COMPARE TO SIMILAR SPECIES: Lack of black coloration on lower belly, dull blue-gray legs and bill, and bright tan chest and belly all distinguish from Black-bellied Whistling-Duck.

DID YOU KNOW? Throughout some of its range in South America and Africa, this species is hunted for its perceived negative impact on the rice harvest. Fulvous Whistling-Ducks are known to eat both adjacent weeds and the cereal crop itself during their stays in agricultural fields.

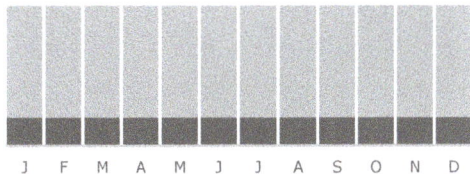

J F M A M J J A S O N D

① **ROYAL TERN.** *Thalasseus maximus.*

SIZE: 19 in.

HABITAT: Oceanic coastlines, particularly sheltered bays and estuaries.

WILD DIET: Mostly small fish (e.g., anchovies), also small crabs and shrimp.

BEHAVIOR: Frequently flies near shore when foraging, preferring calmer stretches of water. When suitable prey is sighted, the tern will hover with wings outstretched as it prepares to plunge headfirst. Interestingly, this hunting technique is modified when dealing with crabs and flying fish; in these instances, the chasseur must instead swoop low over the water as it makes a stealthier approach.

MIGRATE? Partially.

NESTING: Colonial nester, usually on beaches or islands. A spartan affair, a nest scrape is lined with little to no vegetation. Depth may be less than 1 in.

EGGS: Light brown, blue, or olive with dark mottling and/or smudging. Length of 2 ½ in. Total of 1-2.

FEEDER BEHAVIOR: Does not visit feeders.

COMPARE TO SIMILAR SPECIES: Long, pointed bill characteristic of terns, in addition to bright orange bill coloration and streamlined head profile, quickly distinguish from gulls. Among terns, only the Caspian Tern is of similarly large size. The Royal lacks the Caspian's fully dark underwing feathers at the tips (usually just a dark outline on the edges), and has a white forehead from late summer through winter. It is also of slightly daintier profile.

DID YOU KNOW? Though terns are known to suffer from *kleptoparasitism*, or the stealing of prey after capture by another species, the Royal Tern has itself been observed harrying pelicans—which outweigh the tern by an approximate factor of eight—for an easy catch.

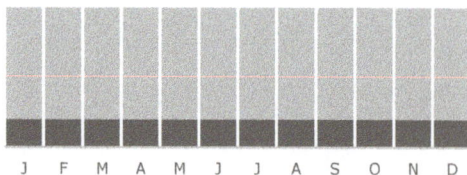

J F M A M J J A S O N D

Nonbreeding adults (Notice bare forehead) at top,
Breeding adult scanning water at bottom (Photo by Melissa McMasters / CC BY-SA / Cropped).

Perching adult at top (Photo by Becky Matsubara / CC BY-SA / Cropped),
Flying adult at bottom.

③ **AMERICAN CROW.** *Corvus brachyrhynchos.*

SIZE: 19 in.
HABITAT: Nearly anywhere, but especially open woods.
WILD DIET: Nearly anything, including nuts and fruits, grains and seeds, eggs and hatchlings, insects and spiders, worms, mice, carrion, and garbage.
BEHAVIOR: Highly intelligent. Engages in sophisticated communication, problem-solving, and self-governing behavior in groups. Often observed in flocks, also known as murders (e.g., a murder of crows).
MIGRATE? No.
NESTING: Hidden in a fork near the trunk of a tree, and near the tree's apex. Cup-shaped, formed from twigs and lined with vegetation. Usually about 1 ft. wide and 6 in. deep.
EGGS: Shades of blue-green, with speckling. Length of 1 ½ in. Total of 3-6.

BIRD FEEDING TIPS

FEEDER DIET: Black-oil and hulled sunflower seeds, suet, oats, cracked corn, peanuts and peanut hearts, millet, milo, fruit. **FEEDER TYPES**: Ground, platforms. **FEEDER BEHAVIOR**: Large size may intimidate some birds upon arrival. Tends to have a large appetite, which proves problematic for some feeder setups, and may take excess food to store elsewhere.

COMPARE TO SIMILAR SPECIES: Most similar to Common Raven, but smaller. Smooth head and throat feathers, while tail is more fan-shaped than wedge-shaped when unfurled. Also, note the characteristic *caw, caw* calls which are familiar across much of the U.S.

DID YOU KNOW? Among many other examples of tool use, crows have taken discarded, still-lit cigarettes and rubbed them inside of their wings to kill parasites; sharpened sticks to poke between fence posts, so as to feed on hidden insects, seeds, and grains; and rewarded humans who set out food with shiny trinkets that they carried from nearby.

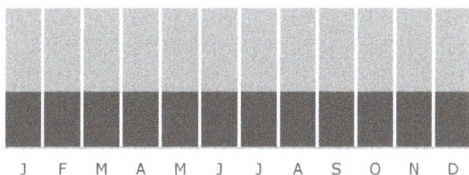

J F M A M J J A S O N D

① AMERICAN OYSTERCATCHER.
Haematopus palliatus.

SIZE: 18 in.

HABITAT: Oceanic coastlines, including nearby islands. Specifically, muddy tidal flats, beaches, and saltmarshes.

WILD DIET: Oysters, mussels, clams. Occasionally, starfish, crabs, sea urchins, and worms.

BEHAVIOR: Walks or darts deliberately in the shallows or on beaches, with frequent investigative pauses as it seeks out its prey. When dealing with bivalves (i.e., two-shelled mollusks, such as clams), it must swiftly insert its bill in the opening between the prey's shells and sever its adductor muscles; if this is not accomplished sufficiently quickly, the mollusk exacts its revenge by tightly grasping the oystercatcher's bill and anchoring it in place, amid the omnipresent dangers of changing tides. Outside of hunting hours, individuals are frequently observed preening their feathers.

MIGRATE? No.

NESTING: Located on beaches or near saltmarshes. An impression is formed in the sand roughly the size of the bird's underside. About 8 in. across.

EGGS: Off-white with brown speckling. Length of 2 - 2 ½ in. Total of 2-3.

FEEDER BEHAVIOR: Does not visit feeders.

COMPARE TO SIMILAR SPECIES: Highly distinctive among oceanic shorebirds, particularly owing to its bright red bill.

DID YOU KNOW? Individual oystercatchers often perfect their own brand of confronting prey. Some use their bills as levers to open shells, and others attempt to break apart the protective shell—with varying degrees of caution appearing to be used with each method.

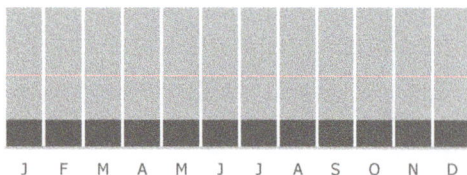

J F M A M J J A S O N D

Adults at top and bottom.

Perching adult at top (Photo by Mosharaf Hossain / CC BY-SA / Cropped),
Flying adult at bottom (Photo by Andy Reago, Chrissy McClarren / CC BY-SA / Cropped).

① PEREGRINE FALCON. *Falco peregrinus.*

SIZE: 18 in.
HABITAT: Coastlines, mountains and valleys, and cities.
WILD DIET: Mostly medium-sized birds (e.g., pigeons, ducks, and gulls); also bats.
BEHAVIOR: Often watching for prey from an elevated perch or from high in the sky. Once prey is sighted, this bird enters a steep dive, reaching speeds of over 240 mph, culminating in a quick strike-and-kill. May also pursue prey from lower heights, flying up to 70 mph horizontally in pursuit: though cruising speeds are often just 30 to 40 mph. Individuals may periodically specialize in certain modes of hunting, depending on dietary needs and habitat characteristics. Some have been known to regularly soar high and dive upon Blue Jays, producing a puff of airborne feathers upon impact, while others have perched near inlets of bays, eagerly awaiting flocks of coots or ducks to unsuspectingly approach. Peregrines are increasingly taking up residence in urban environments, where they hunt pigeons and regularly nest on skyscraper ledges, the latter simulating its natural preference for cliffside nesting.
MIGRATE? Yes.
NESTING: Cliffside ledges. The topsoil is scraped away to form a shallow indentation. About 8 in. across.
EGGS: Off-white to red-brown, with splotchiness. Length of 2 in. Total of 2-4.
FEEDER BEHAVIOR: Does not visit feeders.

COMPARE TO SIMILAR SPECIES: Pointed, swept-back wings differentiate from other birds of prey, such as hawks or eagles. Among falconids, much larger than the Merlin and American Kestrel.

DID YOU KNOW? Like a guided missile, the Peregrine Falcon is able to make minute, controlled adjustments to the direction and camber of its dive to more accurately strike its moving targets. Aeronautical engineers have studied these characteristics for decades in order to understand the potential applications for aircraft, drones, and missiles. This is an example of *biomimicry*, wherein human engineering is modelled after materials or behaviors observed in the animal kingdom—which makes plenty of sense, considering the degree of specialization that each animal must possess to best exploit its well-honed ecological niche.

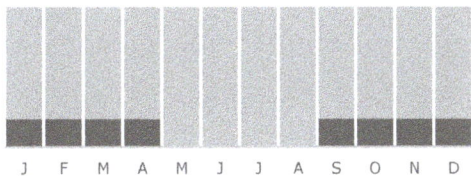

J F M A M J J A S O N D

① BLACK SKIMMER. *Rynchops niger.*

SIZE: 18 in.

HABITAT: Oceanic coastlines and bays. Occasionally present in nearby wetlands.

WILD DIET: Small fish (e.g., anchovies, herring), shrimp, and crabs.

BEHAVIOR: Skimmers feed by flying slightly above the water surface with long bill open and head extended; the mandible, or lower section of bill, is held below the surface in search of small prey. This tactile approach to hunting is highly unique, and the Black Skimmer is able to snap its jaws shut in a fraction of second once any potential prey makes contact with the lower bill. This species' hunting technique requires relatively calm waters to avoid buffeting by heavy waves, and individuals have been observed feeding at all times of day and night, but particularly at sunrise and sunset. Low wing-loading allows for graceful flight.

MIGRATE? No.

NESTING: Loose colonial nester. Selects a beachside location on a protected section of coastline or island. May cohabitate with various species of tern. A shallow impression is scraped into the sand or soil, upon which eggs are laid. About 8 in. across.

EGGS: Off-white, with dark splotches. Length of 2 in. Total of 2-5.

FEEDER BEHAVIOR: Does not visit feeders.

COMPARE TO SIMILAR SPECIES: Highly distinctive among other seabirds, particularly once bill is observed.

DID YOU KNOW? The tendency of Black Skimmers to hunt in twilight, also known as *crepuscularity*, is shared by some other avian species, such as the Chimney Swift and American Woodcock. This may confer this species an advantage when sharing particularly active hunting grounds with other birds which instead hunt primarily by light.

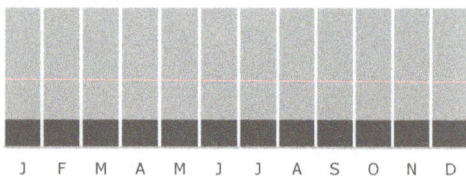

J F M A M J J A S O N D

Adult at top (Photo by Andreas Trepte / CC BY-SA / Cropped)
Adults skimming at bottom.

Male at top,
Male and female at bottom.

① **HOODED MERGANSER.** *Lophodytes cucullatus.*

SIZE: 18 in.
HABITAT: Wetlands, ponds, small lakes and rivers. Occasionally, coastal bays.
WILD DIET: Mostly fish and aquatic invertebrates. Also, small amphibians, insects, and aquatic vegetation.
BEHAVIOR: This species typically congregates in small groups on protected bodies of water, irregularly diving beneath the surface to forage for prey. When diving, the merganser half-leaps from its floating position into the water, producing a clean entrance with minimal surface disturbance—which is important for maintaining its cover when hunting. This duck is able to change directions quickly while underwater, and even observe its surroundings in the most turbid of conditions. Like other mergansers, this species has minute serrations on the lining of its bill, which assist with grasping and securing underwater prey.
MIGRATE? Yes.
NESTING: Cavity nester, using natural or woodpecker-manufactured hollows in trees, as well as nest boxes. Lined with feathers. Entrance less than 6 in. wide.
EGGS: White to off-white, and somewhat spherical. Length of 2 in. Total of 7-13.
FEEDER BEHAVIOR: Does not visit feeders, but uses nest boxes.

COMPARE TO SIMILAR SPECIES: Males have a white head marking resembling that of the Bufflehead, but the rest of its markings are very different. Females may vaguely resemble other merganser species, but Hoodeds are much smaller and possess a more noticeable tuft at the rear of the head.

DID YOU KNOW? Hooded Mergansers have been observed repeatedly throughout the past decade in Dublin, Ireland, but it is likely that these are captive escapees and that they have not yet established a viable breeding population.

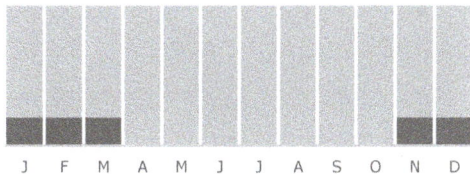

J F M A M J J A S O N D

③ PILEATED WOODPECKER. *Dryocopus pileatus.*

SIZE: 18 in.

HABITAT: Dense, mature woods. Sometimes, semi-open woods and wooded suburbs.

WILD DIET: Mostly insects (in particular, carpenter ants), also some nuts and fruits.

BEHAVIOR: Clings to tree bark while boring into the wood. Individuals may excavate deeply into the trunk, forming ovaline hollows recognizable long after the woodpecker has passed through. These forays are often intended to root out ant colonies; the woodpecker's long, extensible tongue is highly sensitive, and acts both as a tactile antenna and a dexterous tool for rooting out food sources (*See* Photo at bottom left). Occasionally forages at ground level. Likely sparse across its habitat, as individual breeding pairs aggressively defend a territory of several hundred acres from other conspecifics: with loud drilling often used as a signaling mechanism to potential rivals.

MIGRATE? No.

NESTING: Inside dead trees, where a round-entranced cavity is bored 1-2 ft. deep.

EGGS: Milky white with light spotting. Length of 1 ¼ in. Total of 3-5.

BIRD FEEDING TIPS

FEEDER DIET: Suet, black-oil and hulled sunflower seeds, peanuts, mealworms. **FEEDER TYPES**: Suet cages. **FEEDER BEHAVIOR**: Hammers its bill against the suet to dislodge bite-size pieces. Other birds may initially fly away if startled by its arrival.

COMPARE TO SIMILAR SPECIES: Size and distinctive head markings contrast with those of other woodpeckers.

DID YOU KNOW? Pileated Woodpeckers rarely reuse the same nest cavity. This allows many other cavity-nesting birds, many of which are not able to drill their own cavities, to use the hole for nests in future years.

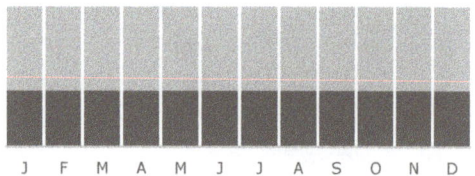

J F M A M J J A S O N D

Adults at top and bottom.

Adults at top and bottom.

① **GREEN HERON.** *Butorides virescens.*

SIZE: 17 in.

HABITAT: Wetlands and ponds, sometimes edges of reservoirs and small lakes.

WILD DIET: Mainly small fish. Also, frogs, insects and spiders, small rodents, and aquatic invertebrates.

BEHAVIOR: A solitary hunter at dusk and dawn, usually remaining somewhat secretive during the day. This species is often observed perched motionless on the edge of the water or in the shallows, waiting for prey to approach. Individuals may also rest aboveground in dense tangles of branches. Suburbanites very occasionally observe these birds flying between foraging locations, with somewhat quick, labored wingbeats, head tucked back, and legs outstretched behind.

MIGRATE? No.

NESTING: Hidden amid dense cover in the crotch of a tree, usually near wetland habitat. Twigs are used to weave a sturdy bowl. About 1 ft. in diameter.

EGGS: Light blue-green. Length of 1 ½ in. Total of 2-5, occasionally with a second brood.

FEEDER BEHAVIOR: Does not visit feeders.

COMPARE TO SIMILAR SPECIES: Dark green back and head, chestnut-colored chest, yellow legs, and partially yellow bill distinguish from other herons and bitterns. Juveniles are buffier all over with a dark head crown.

DID YOU KNOW? The Green Heron is known for exhibiting remarkable feats of intelligence. It sometimes bait-fishes by finding a piece of bread, an insect, or a colorful object to drop on the water's surface; fish are attracted to the decoy and immediately snatched by the heron. Locations where Green Herons have used bread are also frequented by fishermen; consequently, scientists believe that these clever birds may have learned to bait-fish by direct observation of humans.

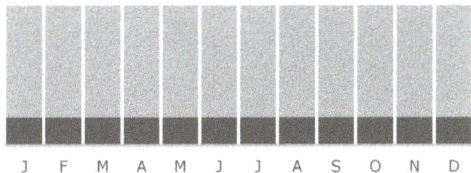

J F M A M J J A S O N D

① LESSER SCAUP (or LITTLE BLUEBILL).
Aythya affinis.

SIZE: 17 in.

HABITAT: Bays of oceans and large lakes, also smaller bodies of water. Breeds in wetlands, usually in Canada or Alaska, as well as in the northwest-central U.S.

WILD DIET: Aquatic invertebrates, also insects and aquatic vegetation.

BEHAVIOR: Usually dives for food in water less than 10 feet deep, but can dive up to 25 feet beneath the surface. These dives may last over a minute, and foraging is conducted by dragging its bill purposefully through the substrate. May be found in medium to large flocks, sometimes with the similarly colored Greater Scaup, as well as the Canvasback or Redhead.

MIGRATE? Yes.

NESTING: Nests on the water or on next to the water's edge, using floating vegetation or tangled grasses, respectively. Typically takes the shape of a shallow bowl.

EGGS: Light brown to olive. Length of 2 - 2 ½ in. Total of 6-13.

FEEDER BEHAVIOR: Does not visit feeders.

COMPARE TO SIMILAR SPECIES: Most similar to the slightly larger Greater Scaup. Greater Scaup males have tinges of green, rather than purple, in their dark head plumage, and may be brighter white on the sides of the belly. Both sexes of Greater have a smoothly rounded head crown, while the Lesser's tapers to a point near the rear of the crown.

DID YOU KNOW? Lesser and Greater Scaups, as well as some other diving duck species in the Great Lakes, have been adversely affected by the rapid spread of the invasive zebra mussel. This mollusk from eastern Europe is known to act as a biological sponge for many toxins, such as selenium. Scaups with a diet high in zebra mussels—and, consequently, selenium—have struggled with infertility, as well as other issues.

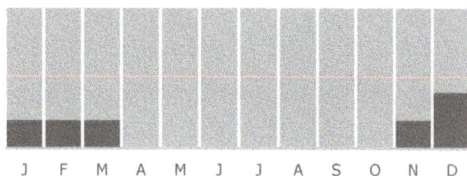

J F M A M J J A S O N D

Male at top,
Female at bottom.

Close-up of male at top,
Two males with female at bottom.

① **RING-NECKED DUCK.** *Aythya collaris.*

SIZE: 17 in.
HABITAT: Wetlands and shallow lakes, ponds. Breeds in wetlands.
WILD DIET: Mostly aquatic vegetation, also aquatic invertebrates and insects.
BEHAVIOR: This species favors the shallows—fully diving beneath the surface as it forages throughout the water column. Compared to many of the dabbling ducks which share their shallow, aquatic habitats, these brief dives enable the Ring-necked Duck to reach vegetation otherwise out of reach for many other species. Sometimes flocks in very large groups, but also may be found in small groups of under a dozen. Mature individuals seem to prefer vegetation to a mixed, omnivorous diet.
MIGRATE? Yes.
NESTING: Nests directly on the water, forming a loose, makeshift bowl of twigs, stems, and grasses atop floating mats of vegetation. About 1 -1 ½ ft. across.
EGGS: Light brown. Length of 2 in. Total of 6-12.
FEEDER BEHAVIOR: Does not visit feeders.

COMPARE TO SIMILAR SPECIES: Most similar to the Greater and Lesser Scaup (which, it must be noted, tend to frequent larger bodies of water, such as bays), but male's feathery tuft atop the crown, black back, white markings up the side of the chest, and ring across bill are distinctive. Females are best identified by a light ring across the bill and a light eye-ring.

DID YOU KNOW? The Ring-necked Duck is named for the scarcely visible reddish-brown ring around the neck of males; this is typically only observable upon careful inspection at a close distance. In the early days of identification, observers would fire upon birds with shotguns and directly approach any fallen individuals—making finer details, such as the ring about this species' neck, much more visible. With binoculars not widely available before the late 1800s, this was the only manner by which most naturalists could accurately identify many of the birds they encountered.

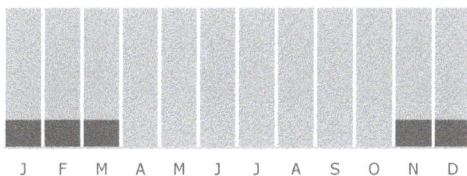

J F M A M J J A S O N D

LARGE BIRDS (12 - 18")

④ **LAUGHING GULL.** *Leucophaeus atricilla.*

SIZE: 16 in.

HABITAT: Oceanic coastlines. Also, sometimes in nearby wetlands, lakes, grain fields, or landfills. Usually not observed more than 25 miles from the coast.

WILD DIET: Diverse and adaptable. Includes insects and invertebrates, garbage, food handouts (though this is not recommended), and even roadkill.

BEHAVIOR: Flocks in large groups, sometimes numbering in the thousands. This species may be accompanied by other gull or tern species. Laughing Gulls lead a boisterous and opportunistic livelihood, noisily chattering with their characteristic *ha-ha-ha...* calls and investigating potential food sources. Individuals are often quite bold toward humans in locations where there is regular interaction.

MIGRATE? Partially.

NESTING: Colonial nesters in coastal saltmarshes, on beaches, and on islands. A semi-woven thatching of vegetation is used to constructed a bowl. About 1 ft. across and 1-3 in. deep.

EGGS: Brown or light blue-green, with mottling. Length of 2 in. Total of 2-4.

FEEDER BEHAVIOR: Does not visit feeders.

COMPARE TO SIMILAR SPECIES: Most similar to the Bonaparte's Gull, which shares territory with the Laughing across much of the Atlantic seaboard, and the Franklin's Gull, which passes through the western reaches of its territory during migration. The Bonaparte's shares the black hood during breeding season, but has a far more petite bill and is of smaller size; during nonbreeding season, it has a defined black ear spot rather than the smudging of the Laughing. The Franklin's shares the black hood during breeding season, but has conspicuous white wingtip spotting at this time (rather than black folded wingtips); it retains a partial black hood near the back of the head during nonbreeding season.

DID YOU KNOW? When formalizing this species' scientific name, the Swedish taxonomist Carl Linnaeus mistakenly named it *atricilla* (black-tailed) instead of *atricapilla* (black-haired), a clear error given this bird's black head and white tail.

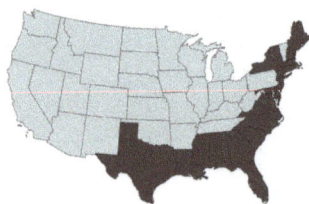

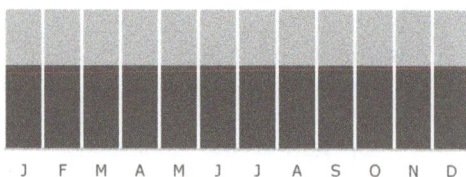

J F M A M J J A S O N D

Nonbreeding adult at top,
Breeding adult at bottom.

Adult at top,
Juvenile at bottom (Photo by Tony Alter / CC BY-SA / Cropped).

② **COOPER'S HAWK.** *Accipiter cooperii.*

SIZE: 16 in.

HABITAT: Dense or open woods, suburbs.

WILD DIET: Mostly medium-sized birds (e.g., doves, robins, and jays), but also small rodents.

BEHAVIOR: Accustomed to deftly flying through cluttered woodland in search of prey. When pursuing its quarry, individuals will hopscotch among concealed perches before briskly swooping at all manner of angles to secure its catch. Its relatively short wings are extremely well adapted for this agile, close-quarters maneuvering, rather than the long gliding favored by many hawks of open country.

MIGRATE? Partially.

NESTING: Situated in large trees, 25-60 ft. above the ground. Platform composed of sticks, with small indentation in the center for eggs. About 2 ft. across and 1 ft. deep.

EGGS: Very light blue. Length of 2 in. Total of 3-5.

FEEDER BEHAVIOR: Often hunts at feeders, particularly if seed is present on the ground (so as to attract ground-feeding prey birds). After a sequence of attacks, it may take several days for feeder activity to fully return to previous levels.

COMPARE TO SIMILAR SPECIES: Longer tail, head-cap markings, coloration, and habitat selection usually differentiate from Red-tailed and Red-shouldered Hawks. Defined dark cap on top of head, as well as often larger size, differentiate adults from adult Sharp-shinned Hawks. Larger size and more defined, mocha-brown markings on chest differentiate juveniles from juvenile Sharp-shinned Hawks.

DID YOU KNOW? Given their penchant for weaving among trees beneath the forest canopy, as many as one-third of all individuals suffer fractures of bones in the chest at some point in their lives, though these wounds tend to recalcify in time.

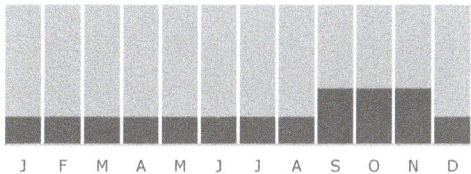

J F M A M J J A S O N D

123

② **BLUE-WINGED TEAL.** *Anas discors.*

SIZE: 16 in.

HABITAT: Wetlands, sometimes ponds and agricultural fields.

WILD DIET: Mostly aquatic vegetation, also aquatic invertebrates and insects. May opportunistically feed in grain (especially rice) fields.

BEHAVIOR: A dabbling duck, this species periodically upends itself as it forages just below the water's surface. Can be very adaptable in its choice of habitat and dietary vegetation, moving through a series of flooded fields, mudflats, marshes, and ponds over the weeks of migration or wintering.

MIGRATE? Yes.

NESTING: Selects a location near the borders of wetlands, amid dense, grassy vegetation. A shallow, small depression is scraped into the soil and lined with thick grasses, stems, and feathers. About 8 in. across.

EGGS: Off-white. Length of 2 in. Total of 7-12.

FEEDER BEHAVIOR: Does not visit feeders.

COMPARE TO SIMILAR SPECIES: Male is quite distinctive with its white, crescent-shaped face marking. However, females are best identified by wholly dark-gray bill (separating from other female dabblers). Females also have a well-defined, dark-brown eye line and a paler section of feather coloration near the base of the bill (distinguishing from female Green-winged Teals).

DID YOU KNOW? This species undertakes one of the longer-distance migrations of the North American ducks. Wintering birds from as far away as northern South America can fly to the northern reaches of Canada for breeding. This migratory distance is partly responsible for their late arrival to breeding grounds come springtime, with individuals typically nesting in early May—after most other hens have begun to incubate their future young.

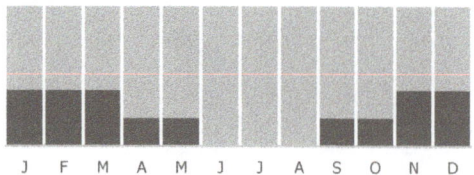

J F M A M J J A S O N D

Male at top,
Females at bottom.

Adults at top, center, and bottom.

② **AMERICAN COOT.** *Fulica americana.*

SIZE: 16 in.

HABITAT: Shorelines of lakes, ponds, and wetlands. Typically found in areas of somewhat dense aquatic vegetation.

WILD DIET: Mostly aquatic vegetation, but sometimes aquatic invertebrates, small fish, and amphibians.

BEHAVIOR: These aquatic, chicken-like birds are often found in flocks of at least a dozen, sometimes many more, and congregate in the shallows on bodies of water of varying size. Foraging is conducted by shallow dives, dabbling, or even standing near the shore or in a few inches of water, plucking algae and grasses with its stubby bill. The coot's lobed toes increase its swimming proficiency, while also preserving its ability to navigate effectively on dry land. Small wings relative to body weight result in a high degree of wing-loading; this is further evidenced by slow, awkward flights and long, running takeoffs. Individuals may loosely associate with some species of ducks.

MIGRATE? Partially.

NESTING: Builds nest overwater on a floating platform of existing aquatic vegetation, weaving together nearby reeds and grasses. About 1 ft. across. Hens often lay eggs in nests of other coots or even those of ducks.

EGGS: Shades of gray or light brown, with dark speckling. Length of 2 in. Total of 5-12, sometimes with a second brood.

FEEDER BEHAVIOR: Does not visit feeders.

COMPARE TO SIMILAR SPECIES: Short, white bill and squat silhouette are very distinctive.

DID YOU KNOW? The American Coot is the namesake for the Toledo Mud Hens, a long-standing Minor League Baseball team. The original ballpark built near the city of Toledo, Ohio was adjacent to vast wetlands inhabited by flocks of coots, and the locals have taken to embracing this unique avian moniker ever since.

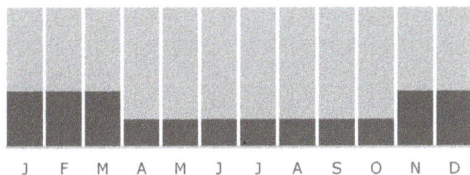

J F M A M J J A S O N D

127

⑤ FISH CROW. *Corvus ossifragus.*

SIZE: 15 in.

HABITAT: Coastlines of oceans, lakes, rivers, and wetlands. Sometimes observed in nearby urban and suburban areas, also grain fields and landfills.

WILD DIET: Crabs, shrimp, bird eggs and hatchlings, sometimes fish. In terrestrial locations, also the following: grains, fruits, reptiles and amphibians, garbage.

BEHAVIOR: Most often associated with the various bodies of water they are known to frequent, the Fish Crow is an opportunistic feeder both in terms of habitat and dietary selection. This species is commonly observed stealing the eggs and fledglings of other birds. Like most corvids (i.e., the family of jays, crows, ravens, etc.), this species possesses an unusual degree of intelligence.

MIGRATE? No.

NESTING: Often nests near treetops. Large bowl of sticks, twigs. About 2 ft. wide.

EGGS: Light blue-green, with dark speckling. Length of 1 ½ in. Total of 3-5.

BIRD FEEDING TIPS

FEEDER DIET: Black-oil and hulled sunflower seeds, suet, oats, cracked corn, peanuts and peanut hearts, millet, milo, fruit. **FEEDER TYPES**: Ground, platforms. **FEEDER BEHAVIOR**: Does not usually visit feeders, but may be present if near a known habitat. Large size and bold attitude may intimidate some birds upon arrival.

COMPARE TO SIMILAR SPECIES: Very similar to American Crow, but slightly smaller (though this is not a reliable indicator) and far more habitat-specific. Best distinguished by voice; the American Crow emits a well-known, bellowing *caw-caw*, while the Fish Crow gives a very nasal *aw-aw* or *uh-uh*.

DID YOU KNOW? Some Fish Crows have been known to wait outside fast food restaurants each day at the time when garbage is taken out, then scavenge for scraps, take the resulting foodstuffs to nearby puddles and birdbaths, and return several hours later once the meal has been better softened for consumption.

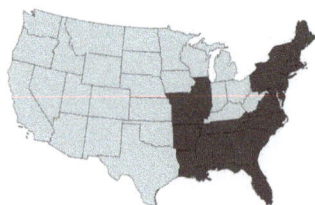

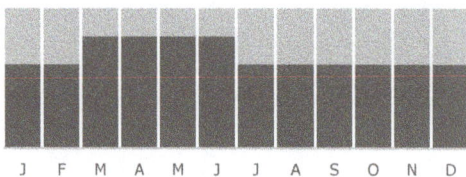

J F M A M J J A S O N D

Adult at top (Photo by Peter W. Chen / CC BY-SA),
Adult at bottom (Photo by Chuck Homler / CC BY-SA / Cropped).

Breeding adult at top left,
Nonbreeding adult at top right,
Nonbreeding adult in flight at bottom (Photo by Mike Baird / CC BY-SA / Cropped).

② **WILLET.** *Tringa semipalmata.*

SIZE: 15 in.

HABITAT: Variety of habitats along oceanic coastlines, including open beaches, sheltered inlets, and tidal zones. During migration, observable in wetlands and flooded fields, as well as on coastlines of larger bodies of water.

WILD DIET: Small crabs, clams, insects (e.g., beetles and insect larvae) and spiders, small fish.

BEHAVIOR: An adaptable forager, this species pursues its prey by a variety of means: methodically walking through the shallows and occasionally pecking throughout the water column, chasing fish and water spiders up to breast-deep, or probing in muddier substrates for invertebrates submerged beneath the visible surface. Except on more crowded wintering grounds, this bird is typically seen on a solitary basis or in lone pairs. So-named for its screechy *pill-will-willet* call.

MIGRATE? Partially.

NESTING: In eastern U.S., typically nests on oceanic shorelines amid the fringes of saltmarshes or atop sand dunes. A shallow bowl of dry grasses and reeds is constructed on the ground. About 6 in. across.

EGGS: Off-white to yellow-brown, with dark mottling. Length of 2 in. Total of 3-4.

FEEDER BEHAVIOR: Does not visit feeders.

COMPARE TO SIMILAR SPECIES: Most similar to Greater and Lesser Yellowlegs, though both of these species lack the distinctive white and black barring across the Willet's wing in flight, have noticeably yellow legs (as the common names would suggest, rather than the pale legs of the Willet), and slightly smaller heads.

DID YOU KNOW? Willets are known to mate for life, returning to the same breeding site each year—a somewhat unusual practice among shorebirds.

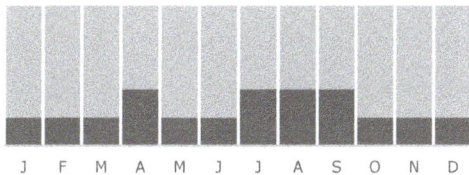

J F M A M J J A S O N D

① **BUFFLEHEAD.** *Bucephala albeola.*

SIZE: 14 in.

HABITAT: Harbors and bays of oceans and the Great Lakes. Sometimes lakes and ponds during migration, and especially during breeding season.

WILD DIET: Almost entirely aquatic invertebrates and insects.

BEHAVIOR: The smallest diving duck in North America, this species dives repeatedly below the surface for intervals of less than a half-minute, and to depths of up to 20 feet. It must take these foraging dives persistently throughout the day in order to sustain its unusually high metabolism. Like other diving ducks, this species is not usually observed walking on land, with the feet set behind each individual's center of mass to best allow for efficient underwater paddling. Furthermore, its diminutive size is specifically adapted to fill a unique ecological niche. While individuals forage in habitats frequented by other diving ducks, they nest almost entirely in cavities left by Northern Flickers, rather than the larger hollows left by Pileated Woodpeckers (which are subject to fierce competition from other, larger cavity-nesting ducks).

MIGRATE? Yes.

NESTING: Breeds in wooded areas near lakes and ponds. Nests in cavities left by Northern Flickers, or in nest boxes. Lined with feathers. Entrance usually less than 4 in. wide.

EGGS: Shiny, milky white. Length of 2 in. Total of 6-12.

FEEDER BEHAVIOR: Does not visit feeders, but sometimes uses nest boxes.

COMPARE TO SIMILAR SPECIES: White chest and belly distinguish males from Hooded Merganser males, and females have a distinctive white mark behind the eye.

DID YOU KNOW? The seemingly large head of this duck led early observers to give it the name of "buffalo head," the portmanteau of which remains this species' common name today. Similarly, the genus name is derived from the Ancient Greek *Bucephalus*, or "ox-headed," which was also the given name of Alexander the Great's valorous, well-renowned warhorse.

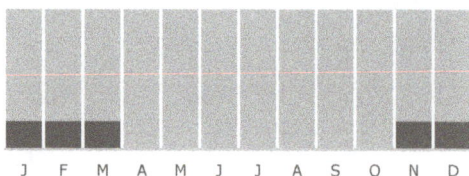

J F M A M J J A S O N D

Male at top (Photo by Mike Pazzani / CC BY-SA / Cropped),
Females at bottom.

Adults at top and bottom.

① **BLACK-NECKED STILT.** *Himantopus mexicanus.*

SIZE: 14 in.
HABITAT: Shallows of wetlands, flooded fields, saturated floodplains.
WILD DIET: Aquatic invertebrates and insects (e.g., crayfish, shrimp, insect larvae, mayflies), small amphibians, small fish.
BEHAVIOR: Slowly wades through the shallows, often no more than a few inches deep. May forage by quickly striking prey after a visual identification, or by tactilely sweeping the bill. When approached too closely, known to suddenly alight to find a new foraging site; this is usually accompanied by loud yipping calls. Fledglings are particularly quick to learn the ropes of the wild—some have been observed darting across the sand or swimming within hours of hatching.
MIGRATE? Partially.
NESTING: Semicolonial nester, with nests separated by dozens of feet but often forming a loose rookery. Selects a site with ample vegetation, and with nearby shallows for foraging. Forms a scrape with light interior lining of dried grasses and solid debris. About 6-8 in. across.
EGGS: Yellow-brown with dark mottling. Length of 2 in. Total of 3-5.
FEEDER BEHAVIOR: Does not visit feeders.

COMPARE TO SIMILAR SPECIES: Regal posture; white throat, eyebrow, and underside; and long, thin, reddish-pink legs are most diagnostic.

DID YOU KNOW? Black-necked Stilts are known for their well-developed and aggressive nest-guarding behaviors. When a threat approaches the nest, a group of stilts will often gather around the potential predator—loudly yipping, jumping about, and aggressively flapping their wings. They have also been known to deceive predators by pretending to incubate decoy nests.

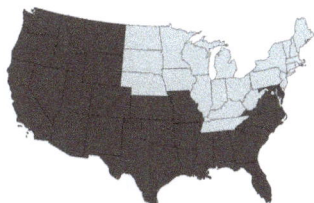

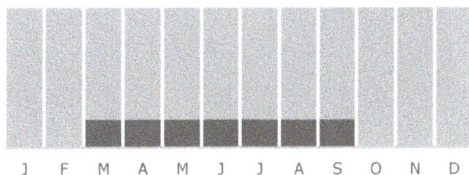

J F M A M J J A S O N D

③ PIED-BILLED GREBE. *Podilymbus podiceps.*

SIZE: 14 in.

HABITAT: Wetlands, ponds, lakes, calmer sections of rivers.

WILD DIET: Mostly crustaceans and small fish (up to 6 in. long). Also, other aquatic invertebrates, insects, and amphibians.

BEHAVIOR: Active divers, grebes are known for their exceptional maneuverability while swimming underwater—on account of large, webbed feet located behind the center of gravity. As a result of this adaptation, individuals tend to be quite ungainly on land and are almost always observed in the water. With graceful, arced leaps, these birds frequently dive below the surface and can reach depths of up to 50 feet repeatedly throughout the day. When surfacing with a small fish, the grebe tosses and spins the catch in its bill, before swallowing it headfirst. Often found in small groups or by themselves, scattered across the surface of the water.

MIGRATE? Partially.

NESTING: Anchored to floating aquatic vegetation, and takes the approximate shape of a platform. Constructed of twigs and stems. Less than 6 in. wide.

EGGS: White. Length of 1 ½ - 2 in. Total of 3-8, sometimes with a second brood.

FEEDER BEHAVIOR: Does not visit feeders.

COMPARE TO SIMILAR SPECIES: Very small size among the waterfowl, and distinctively small and stubby bill relative to other species.

DID YOU KNOW? Grebes, including the Pied-billed, are well-known for consuming their own feathers, which may help with the following: protecting the stomach from indigestible bones or shells, preventing these items from passing to the intestines, or allowing for these indigestible items to be more easily packaged as pellets for regurgitation. In some grebes, the stomach has been observed to be up to half-full with feathered contents.

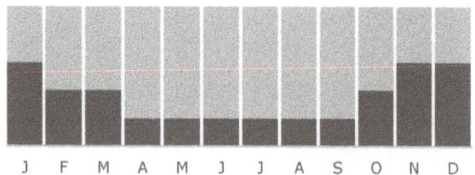

J F M A M J J A S O N D

Breeding adult with juvenile at top,
Nonbreeding adult at bottom.

Adult resting in nonbreeding plumage at top,
Adults in breeding plumage at bottom.

① **FORSTER'S TERN.** *Sterna forsteri.*

SIZE: 14 in.

HABITAT: Coastlines of oceans, lakes, and rivers. Also, (usually expansive) wetlands.

WILD DIET: Mostly small fish (e.g., minnows, sunfish, perch, sardines). Occasionally, flying insects.

BEHAVIOR: A tern which breeds in wetlands during the spring and summer, this species is subsequently found in a wide variety of habitats throughout the balance of the year. When migrating and wintering, larger bodies of water are often inhabited. Like many terns, this species will often fly 15 to 30 feet above the water's surface, scanning for prey before plunge-diving in pursuit; however, unlike many of its relatives, this tern also has a penchant for perching over the water on dock pilings, fencing, or wires and waiting for suitable prey to swim nearby.

MIGRATE? Partially.

NESTING: Colonial nester. Selects a location at ground level amid dense wetland vegetation or even atop floating vegetation. May be a shallow depression or well-defined cup, usually lined with grasses. About 6-9 in. across.

EGGS: Light brown, with dark mottling, speckling. Length of 1 ½ in. Total of 2-4.

FEEDER BEHAVIOR: Does not visit feeders.

COMPARE TO SIMILAR SPECIES: Straight, pointed bill and streamlined profile distinguish from small gulls. This species is very similar to the Forster's Tern in both size and coloration. Differences include the following: the Common has gray upperwing coloration, while the Forster's has silvery white; the Common has darker folded rear wingtips when viewed at rest, while on the Forster's these are light gray or whiteish; and the Common possesses a black nape in fall and winter, while the Forster's instead has a large black spot over the eye.

DID YOU KNOW? Forster's Terns are aggressive in defense of their nests, and some other wetland breeders, such as ducks, grebes, and blackbirds, have been known to nest nearby in order to benefit from the resultant sphere of protection.

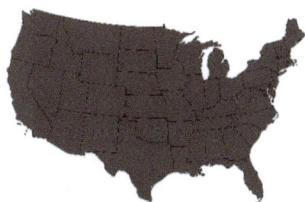

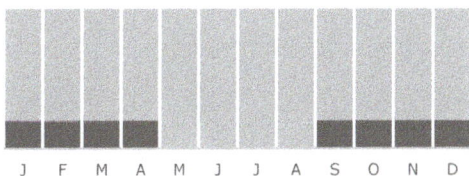

J F M A M J J A S O N D

④ BOAT-TAILED GRACKLE. *Quiscalus major.*

SIZE: 14 in.

HABITAT: Mostly wetlands, sometimes urban areas and fields. Rarely far from saltwater, except in Peninsular Florida.

WILD DIET: Grains, fruits, insects and spiders, worms, reptiles and amphibians, small fish, and garbage.

BEHAVIOR: These birds are perhaps best known for their large populations in and around saltwater wetlands: foraging by probing in the sand, soil, or shallow water for food items. Most individuals will not move more than 25 miles from their birthplace over a lifetime, and will remain within 10 to 25 miles of the oceanic coast. May loosely flock with the Great-tailed Grackle where their ranges overlap.

MIGRATE? No.

NESTING: Located a few feet aboveground in a bush, amid dense wetland vegetation. Occasionally in trees. The nest is a tight cup, woven with twigs and grasses. About 8 in. across.

EGGS: Light brown to light blue-green, with muddy splotches. Length of 1 ½ in. Total of 1-5, with 1-2 broods.

BIRD FEEDING TIPS

FEEDER DIET: Black-oil and hulled sunflower seeds, cracked corn, peanut hearts, millet, safflower seed. **FEEDER TYPES**: Ground, platforms. **FEEDER BEHAVIOR**: Can accumulate in flocks, and aggressive behavior may frighten away other bird species.

COMPARE TO SIMILAR SPECIES: Dark eye distinguishes from the Great-tailed Grackle in TX and LA, in addition to habitat (Boat-taileds rarely wander far from water) and smaller size. Larger with longer tail than the Common Grackle.

DID YOU KNOW? This grackle species possesses loads of intelligence, with individuals frequently spotted retrieving scraps of human food and briefly submerging them in water for easier, less inhibited consumption.

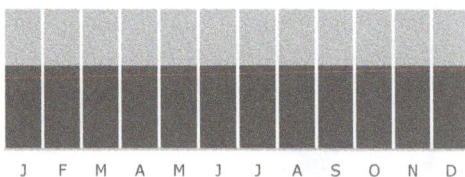

J F M A M J J A S O N D

Male at top,
Female at bottom.

Adult swimming at top,
Adult perched at bottom.

③ COMMON GALLINULE. *Gallinula galeata.*

SIZE: 13 in.

HABITAT: Mostly wetlands and ponds, sometimes edges of lakes. Typically found in areas of somewhat dense aquatic vegetation.

WILD DIET: Aquatic vegetation, insects and spiders, snails, fruits and berries, and amphibians.

BEHAVIOR: Sits high in the water while bobbing its head as it swims, or slowly walks across lily pads and logs while seeking out its next meal. May upend while foraging, or flip over aquatic vegetation for insects or snails hidden beneath. Its long, spindly toes allow for effortless treading across loose, muddy banks or tenuously floating aquatic vegetation. This species is usually secretive, and does not flock in groups—outside of small, familial groups, that is—except in winter.

MIGRATE? No.

NESTING: Builds nest overwater on a floating platform bowl of existing aquatic vegetation, weaving together nearby reeds and grasses. Occasionally nests in low trees. About 1 ft. across.

EGGS: Off-white to light brown, with irregular brown speckling. Length of 2 in. Total of 4-11, sometimes with a second brood.

FEEDER BEHAVIOR: Does not visit feeders.

COMPARE TO SIMILAR SPECIES: Most similar to American Coot, but red on upper bill and forehead, smaller size, and sleeker silhouette are helpful differentiators.

DID YOU KNOW? The Common Gallinule is also found in Hawaii, where it is known as the ʻAlae ʻUla and has experienced steep population declines. It is frequently celebrated in native folklore, with legend suggesting that this "fire-bringer" was responsible for presenting the gift of fire from the heavens to the people, explaining its burnt-red forehead.

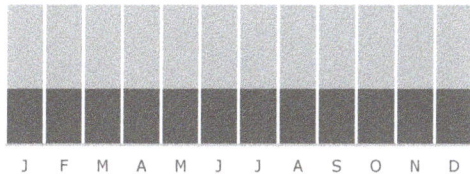

J F M A M J J A S O N D

143

④ **ROCK DOVE (or ROCK PIGEON).**
Columba livia.

SIZE: 13 in.
HABITAT: Urban areas.
WILD DIET: Grains, seeds, berries, and garbage.
BEHAVIOR: Forages on the ground, often in flocks of at least several dozen. Also loiters in parks if there is a consistent source of human-supplied food. While walking along, this species repeatedly nods its head forward, which provides a steadier field of vision by counterbalancing its choppy gait. Large flocks are often observed perched on telephone wires, ledges of buildings, or billboards.
MIGRATE? No.
NESTING: In urban areas, nests in crevices or on ledges of buildings, particularly where there is some overhead shelter. Small platform, constructed with sticks and vegetation. Over time, may grow in size with the accumulated feces of past nesting generations.
EGGS: White. Length of 1 ½ in. Total of 2. Usually raises 3-4 broods each year, but may raise up to 6.

BIRD FEEDING TIPS

FEEDER DIET: Black-oil and hulled sunflower seeds, cracked corn, peanut hearts, millet, safflower seed. **FEEDER TYPES:** Ground, platforms, hoppers. **FEEDER BEHAVIOR:** Most likely to visit if feeders are situated near urban centers, bridges, or overpasses.

COMPARE TO SIMILAR SPECIES: Similar in shape and silhouette to Mourning Dove, but note clear difference in coloration and markings.

DID YOU KNOW? Due to their characteristic homing abilities, domesticated pigeons have long been used to convey messages to distant locations. Rock Doves, in particular, have been used to carry such things as postal messages and wartime communications over distances spanning hundreds—and even thousands—of miles.

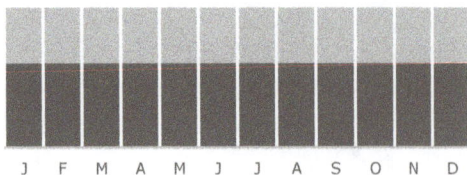

J F M A M J J A S O N D

Adult at top,
Adults in flight at bottom.

Breeding adult at top,
Nonbreeding adult at bottom.

① **GREATER YELLOWLEGS.** *Tringa melanoleuca.*

SIZE: 13 in.

HABITAT: Wetlands, mudflats, flooded fields; also, edges of streams, ponds, reservoirs, lakes.

WILD DIET: Aquatic insects and invertebrates, sometimes fish and small frogs.

BEHAVIOR: Usually observed foraging solitarily, with a slight preference for deeper portions of shallows compared to other shorebirds. Wades through the water or walks across mudflats with a peculiar, high-stepping motion. Known for striking its prey with a quick downward peck or by repeated probing motions: particularly when foraging in more turbid, or opaque, waters. Rather unusually for a shorebird, males may be observed standing sentry over their nesting territories from elevated positions in the treetops, most often during the breeding season.

MIGRATE? Partially.

NESTING: Selects a concealed location amid the dense vegetation at the edges of wetlands. Digs a light scrape in the moss or soil. Up to 6 in. across.

EGGS: Light brown with heavy dark mottling. Length of 2 in. Total of 3-4.

FEEDER BEHAVIOR: Does not visit feeders.

COMPARE TO SIMILAR SPECIES: Large size and conspicuous, bright yellow legs distinguish from most other shorebird species. Lesser Yellowlegs is very similar, but stands a few inches shorter, and has a bill approximately the length of its head (compared to that of the Greater, which is at least one-and-a-half times the length of its head). Also, the bill of the Greater is slightly upturned at the end, though this can be difficult to spot in the field.

DID YOU KNOW? Despite its remarkable similarity with the Lesser Yellowlegs, this species is actually more closely related to the gray-legged Willet. All three species are members of the *Tringa* genus, which was named for an antiquitous shorebird originally described by the Greek polymath Aristotle.

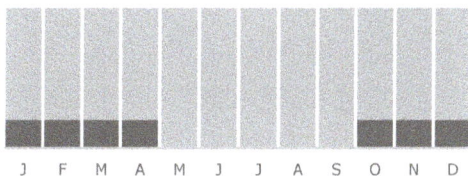

J F M A M J J A S O N D

③ **BELTED KINGFISHER.** *Megaceryle alcyon.*

SIZE: 13 in.

HABITAT: Variety of bodies of water, including bays, lakes, rivers, and ponds. Prefers to hunt over calm, clearer water whenever available.

WILD DIET: Mostly small fish (e.g., trout, perch, sunfish, sticklebacks), sometimes crayfish, snails, amphibians, insects, and small mammals.

BEHAVIOR: This species is often found on the fringes of local ponds and streams, perched atop a post, branch, or wire overlooking the water. When prey is spotted, the kingfisher flies near the targeted location, often hovers momentarily on flapping wings, and plunge-dives bill-first to collect its meal. The catch is then consumed headfirst from a nearby perch. As the kingfisher flies around its habitat, it commonly emits a series of characteristic, rattling calls, which provide a telltale indicator of its nearby presence.

MIGRATE? Yes.

NESTING: Digs a long, hidden burrow into a vertical or steeply sloped earthen bank. About 3-8 ft. deep with an enlarged, elevated nest chamber at the terminus.

EGGS: Bright white. Length of 1 ½ in. Total of 4-8, sometimes with a second brood.

FEEDER BEHAVIOR: Does not visit feeders.

COMPARE TO SIMILAR SPECIES: Very distinctive, there are few birds which resemble this species. In S Texas, the larger Ringed Kingfisher has a more sizable bill and females have a fully orange-red chest and belly; also in S Texas, the smaller Green Kingfisher possesses a dark green cast and lacks the spiky crest of Belted.

DID YOU KNOW? The tricks of the Belted Kingfisher's trade are carefully guarded and passed from generation to generation. Parents teach their young to hunt by dropping dead prey fish in the water for retrieval, allowing the young an opportunity to wet their bills before heading off on their own.

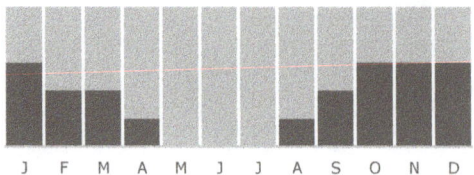

J F M A M J J A S O N D

Male at top,
Female at bottom (Notice presence of chestnut breast coloration).

Adults at top and bottom.

④ EURASIAN COLLARED-DOVE.
Streptopelia decaocto.

SIZE: 12 in.

HABITAT: Cities and suburbs, sometimes agricultural fields.

WILD DIET: Mostly seeds and grains.

BEHAVIOR: A species originally native to wide swaths of the Palearctic, from the British Isles to the Korean Peninsula. A pet shop in the Bahamas released several dozen in 1974, after which populations have made their way into much of North America, gradually hopscotching across cities and grain fields. Often found in flocks, audibly cooing as it forages by pecking for food across the ground.

MIGRATE? No.

NESTING: Almost always within a stone's throw of human habitation. Selects a location in a tree or on a utility pole. Woven bowl of twigs. About 6-8 in. across.

EGGS: Creamy white. Length of 1 in. Total of 1-2. Usually raises 3-4 broods each year, but may raise up to 6.

BIRD FEEDING TIPS

FEEDER DIET: Black-oil and hulled sunflower seeds, cracked corn, millet, milo, peanut hearts, oats. **FEEDER TYPES**: Ground, platforms, hoppers. **FEEDER BEHAVIOR**: Usually announces its arrival with a fluttering of wings as it softens its descent to the ground or feeder. May loiter as it intermittently pecks at feed, often on the ground. Sometimes chases off other species, but this behavior can be seasonal or resource-dependent.

COMPARE TO SIMILAR SPECIES: Dark collar around back of neck is diagnostic.

DID YOU KNOW? Though most birds must tilt their heads back to swallow water, all doves are able to simultaneously swallow while drinking.

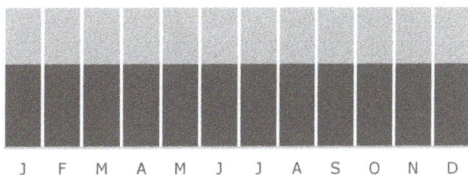

J F M A M J J A S O N D

LARGE BIRDS (12 - 18")

④ **COMMON GRACKLE.** *Quiscalus quiscula.*

SIZE: 12 in.

HABITAT: Open woods, wetlands, fields, and suburbs.

WILD DIET: Seeds, grains, insects and spiders, frogs, eggs, mice, and small birds.

BEHAVIOR: Frequently forages across lawns and fields, and perches in shrubs or atop marsh grasses. Roosts high in trees. When flying in search of another location to scavenge, this species may emit a deep *chek* sound; the long, flowing tail with a diamond-like extension is characteristic of this species and highly recognizable.

MIGRATE? No.

NESTING: In conifers, well above the ground. Often near wetland habitats. Cup-shaped, constructed of grasses and twigs. Up to 12 in. across, and 8 in. tall.

EGGS: Shades of blue or blue-green, with dark mottling. Length of 1 in. Total of 3-6, occasionally with a second brood.

BIRD FEEDING TIPS

FEEDER DIET: Black-oil and hulled sunflower seeds, suet, safflower seed, cracked corn, peanuts and peanut hearts, oats, millet, milo, fruit. **FEEDER TYPES**: Ground, platforms, hoppers. **FEEDER BEHAVIOR**: Can dominate feeders due to their size and attitudes. Often observed foraging on ground, or briefly perching on bark to feed on suet.

COMPARE TO SIMILAR SPECIES: Long tail with diamond-like attachment is largely distinctive among blackbirds of this size. In addition, the European Starling is smaller, has somewhat different markings, and lacks a relatively long tail.

DID YOU KNOW? The flocking tendency and resourcefulness of this species, along with its preference for seeds and grains, has resulted in millions of dollars' worth of damage to agricultural crops, especially corn.

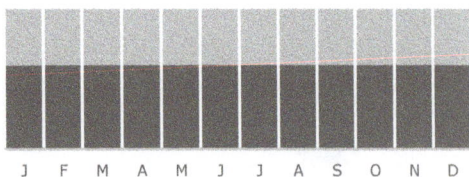

J F M A M J J A S O N D

Male at top,
Female at bottom (Photo by Bob Peterson / CC BY-SA / Cropped).

Adults at top,
Nestlings at bottom.

① **NANDAY PARAKEET (also NANDAY CONURE, or BLACK-HOODED PARAKEET).**
Aratinga nenday.

SIZE: 12 in.

HABITAT: Open woods, including suburbs. May also be observed in denser woods or in cities, depending on food availability.

WILD DIET: Nuts, seeds, fruits, berries, flowers, flower buds, and grains.

BEHAVIOR: Often found in large groups and roosts, noisily squawking from tree branches and utility wires. Usually forages on the ground, but may take fruits or berries directly from branches. Populations are somewhat localized.

MIGRATE? No.

NESTING: Cavity nester, often outcompeting woodpeckers and other cavity nesters for existing nesting sites. Cavities often have openings measuring 4-6 in. across, and an interior about 1 - 1 ½ feet deep.

EGGS: White. Length of 1-1 ½ in. Total of 3-5.

BIRD FEEDING TIPS

FEEDER DIET: Fruit, black-oil and hulled sunflower seeds, safflower seed, cracked corn, peanuts and peanut hearts, oats, millet, milo. **FEEDER TYPES**: Ground, platforms, hoppers. **FEEDER BEHAVIOR**: Only found at feeders in areas with established feral populations. Flocking behavior may sometimes overwhelm feeder stations.

COMPARE TO SIMILAR SPECIES: Among parrots and parakeets, the well-defined black hood and bill are distinctive.

DID YOU KNOW? An invasive species originally native to central South America, releases from the pet trade have established wild populations of this species across Florida as well as in Phoenix, Los Angeles, and some cities in Texas.

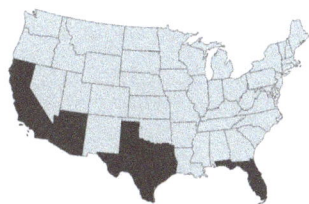

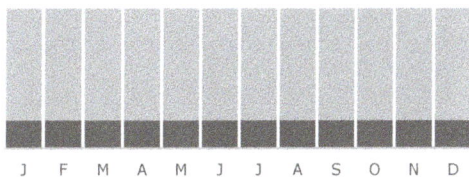

J F M A M J J A S O N D

① SHARP-SHINNED HAWK. *Accipiter striatus.*

SIZE: 12 in.

HABITAT: Dense woods, sometimes wooded suburbs.

WILD DIET: Mostly small to medium-sized songbirds. Rarely, small rodents.

BEHAVIOR: Selects hidden perches at a variety of heights, ambushing prey with quick and stealthy approaches. Often flies nimbly through dense thickets and forest understories when hunting, requiring split-second reflexes and precise, acrobatic movements. As such, this hawk is a member of the accipiters (along with the closely related Cooper's Hawk), which tend to feature short, rounded wings and long, rudder-like tails as express adaptations for this hunting technique.

MIGRATE? Yes.

NESTING: Usually in conifers, well above the ground. Near the top of tree, but beneath the forest canopy. Platform-shaped and constructed with twigs. About 18 in. across and 4 in. deep.

EGGS: Off-white, with variety of bright splotches. Length of 1 ½ in. Total of 4-6.

FEEDER BEHAVIOR: Sometimes hunts at feeders, but less frequently than the Cooper's Hawk.

COMPARE TO SIMILAR SPECIES: Adults are superficially similar to the Cooper's Hawk, but smaller size, lack of well-defined dark cap on head, and habitat choice are often helpful differences. Juveniles are separated from juvenile Cooper's by less-defined, splotchier, and tawnier chest markings.

DID YOU KNOW? Though one of the more secretive hawks found in North America, this species spectacularly travels en masse during migration, sometimes even overwhelming experienced hawk-watchers. As many as 10,000 individuals have been counted in a single day in some locations—the most productive of which tend to be situated along prominent coastlines or mountain ridges.

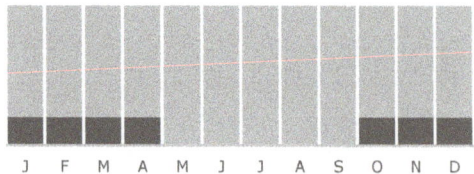

J F M A M J J A S O N D

Adult at left,
Juvenile at right.

Adult perched at top,
Three adults with two Eurasian Collared Doves (left) at bottom: notice white wing fringes.

① WHITE-WINGED DOVE. *Zenaida asiatica.*

SIZE: 12 in.

HABITAT: Desert scrub, cities and suburbs, grain fields.

WILD DIET: Mostly seeds and grains, also fruits.

BEHAVIOR: Historical range mirrored that of the saguaro cactus, on which this species is known to partially depend for seed and fruit supply throughout late spring and summer. Recently, however, this species has expanded its range northward in line with increased numbers of bird feeders and agricultural processing facilities, as well as due to global warming. Coos and forages both on the ground and in trees or shrubs; also exhibits a slower eating motion than the familiar, rapid pecking of Mourning or Rock Doves.

MIGRATE? No.

NESTING: In towns, often found in branches under shade of large trees. In scrubland, often colonially near streams or rivers. Shallow platform bowl of twigs. About 6 in. across.

EGGS: White. Length of 1 in. Total of 1-2, with 1-3 broods.

BIRD FEEDING TIPS

FEEDER DIET: Black-oil and hulled sunflower seeds, cracked corn, millet, milo, oats. **FEEDER TYPES**: Platforms, ground, hoppers. **FEEDER BEHAVIOR**: More likely than other, larger doves to prefer platforms or hoppers, though it will readily take feed from the ground. Feeder activity may wax and wane with wild fruit crops and migratory cycles.

COMPARE TO SIMILAR SPECIES: Similar to other doves, particularly the Mourning Dove, but differences include the following: broad, lateral white wing bars in flight; white fringes of folded wings; broad, rather than tapered, feathered tail; and plain, rather than partially spotted, upper side.

DID YOU KNOW? Migratory and dietary patterns in this species have been tracked by isotope analysis of its feathers; from this information, unique signatures of various geographies and even that of the saguaro—a popular dietary item—can be inferred.

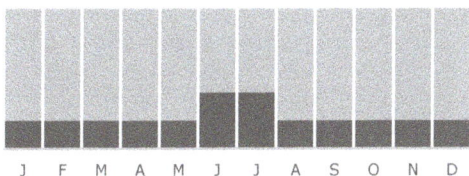

J F M A M J J A S O N D

159

MEDIUM TO LARGE BIRDS (8 ½ - 12")

① **NORTHERN FLICKER.** *Colaptes auratus.*

SIZE: 12 in.

HABITAT: Open woods, fields, and suburbs.

WILD DIET: Mostly insects and spiders (in particular, ants). Also, seeds and berries.

BEHAVIOR: These uniquely patterned woodpeckers are the only species of their kind which routinely feeds on the ground. Ant hills are often sought, and this species' long, nimble tongue is able to extend several inches from its bill to collect larvae and mature ants alike. If present in agricultural pastures, this bird may also hammer apart cow dung in order to feast on any insects present inside.

MIGRATE? Partially.

NESTING: Excavated holes in dead tree trunks or large branches. May be reused from other species. Exterior hole is about 3-4 in. in diameter, and cavity is over 1 ft. deep.

EGGS: White. Length of 1 in. Total of 5-6, sometimes with a second brood.

BIRD FEEDING TIPS

FEEDER DIET: Suet, black-oil and hulled sunflower seeds, safflower seed, cracked corn, peanuts and peanut hearts, millet. **FEEDER TYPES**: Suet cages, ground, platforms, hoppers. **FEEDER BEHAVIOR**: Less common at feeders, but usually observed consuming suet from a cage, or scavenging on the ground.

COMPARE TO SIMILAR SPECIES: Coloration and spotted patterning are distinctive among woodpeckers. Much stouter, thicker neck than doves or robins.

DID YOU KNOW? During the breeding season, dueling males may engage in a bill-sparring match which roughly resembles the Olympic sport of fencing. The prospective female watches from a safe distance—awaiting the winner and soon-to-be mate.

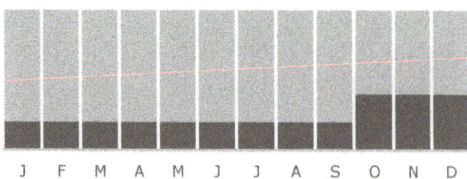

J F M A M J J A S O N D

Adults at top and bottom.

Breeding adult at top,
Nonbreeding adult at bottom.

① **LESSER YELLOWLEGS.** *Tringa flavipes.*

SIZE: 12 in.

HABITAT: Wetlands, mudflats, flooded fields; also, edges of streams, ponds, reservoirs, and lakes.

WILD DIET: Aquatic insects and invertebrates, sometimes fish and small frogs.

BEHAVIOR: Stalks through the shallows of its wetland habitat, occasionally increasing pace or pecking beneath the surface when prey is spotted. Like the Greater Yellowlegs, it also walks with a high-stepping gait and may wade up to its chest while foraging. This allows for individuals to exploit sections of wetland unsuitable for smaller shorebirds, such as Spotted or Least Sandpipers. When foraging, usually present by itself or in very small, scattered numbers. Hatchlings are precocious, leaving the nest within hours and effectively presenting a model of self-sufficiency.

MIGRATE? Partially.

NESTING: Well-concealed locations in the vicinity of its typical wetland habitat, often amid dense vegetation or debris. Digs a light scrape in the moss or soil. About 3-4 in. across.

EGGS: Light brown with heavy dark mottling. Length of 1 ½ - 2 in. Total of 3-4.

FEEDER BEHAVIOR: Does not visit feeders.

COMPARE TO SIMILAR SPECIES: Medium-large size and conspicuous, bright yellow legs distinguish from most other shorebird species. Greater Yellowlegs is very similar, but stands a few inches taller, and has a bill at least one-and-a-half times the length of its head (compared to that of the Lesser, which is about the length of its head).

DID YOU KNOW? When flushed, this wary shorebird usually gives a one- or two-note squeaking call, rather than the more forceful three- or four-note call of the Greater Yellowlegs. To better recall this difference, consider that the Lesser Yellowlegs gives a "lesser" number of notes.

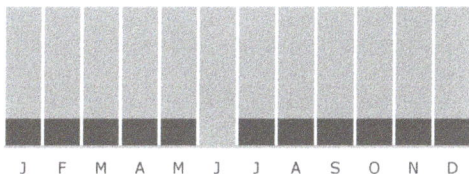

J F M A M J J A S O N D

⑤ MOURNING DOVE. *Zenaida macroura.*

SIZE: 12 in.

HABITAT: Open woods, fields, suburbs, roadsides.

WILD DIET: Various seeds.

BEHAVIOR: Often observed perching on wires, fences, roofs, and in trees, while repeatedly *hooing* with its signature, melancholy call. Pecks for food on the ground, and is not an overly picky eater. To accompany its voracious appetite for seeds, this species swallows fine rocks or sands to aid in digestion. Occasionally may be observed sunning itself on the ground, with wings and tail splayed out.

MIGRATE? No.

NESTING: Hidden among tree branches, in shrubs, on the ground, or in artificial objects such as eaves and gutters. Cup-shaped, and constructed with conifer needles, grasses, and small sticks. About 8 in. across.

EGGS: White. Length of 1 in. Total of 2. Usually raises 2-3 broods each year, but may raise up to 6.

BIRD FEEDING TIPS

FEEDER DIET: Black-oil and hulled sunflower seeds, safflower seed, cracked corn, peanut hearts, millet, oats, nyjer, milo. **FEEDER TYPES**: Ground, platforms, hoppers. **FEEDER BEHAVIOR**: May rest or forage beneath feeders. Common prey for feeder-raiding Cooper's Hawks, and sometimes Sharp-shinned or even Red-shouldered Hawks.

COMPARE TO SIMILAR SPECIES: Much paler than Rock Doves, and usually found in less urban areas. Tapered, feathered tails are easily observable when perching, which are very different from the more rectangular tails of Sharp-shinned Hawks and American Kestrels, not to mention many other visual differences.

DID YOU KNOW? Occasionally called turtle doves, these birds are anything but slow in flight—reaching speeds of up to 55 mph as they whistle through the air.

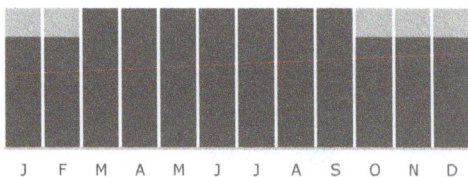

J F M A M J J A S O N D

Adult on ground at top,
Adult perched on wire at bottom (Photo by Heide Couch / CC BY-SA / Cropped).

Adults at top and bottom.

① YELLOW-BILLED CUCKOO.
Coccyzus americanus.

SIZE: 11 in.

HABITAT: Moderately open to dense woods, often with thickets.

WILD DIET: Mostly caterpillars. At times, insects and spiders, small fruits, seeds.

BEHAVIOR: Patiently shrouds itself from view amid forest foliage, waiting for caterpillars or other insects to make their presence known. Migrates roughly in accord with butterfly and moth breeding cycles, and winters in South America. When its preferred prey is sparse, may be observed sallying out to grab flying insects on the wing or gleaning fruits from bushes. When it navigates between perches, flight is direct and quick, with heavy beats of its pointed, slightly backswept wings. Aside from its participation in breeding behavior, individuals are most often solitary.

MIGRATE? Yes.

NESTING: Nests on the sturdy branch of a tree (e.g., oak, ash, beech) or bush. Cup of woven twigs. About 6-8 in. across. Occasionally, lays eggs in nests of other species, particularly those of the closely related Black-billed Cuckoo.

EGGS: Light blue-green. Length of 1 - 1 ½ in. Total of 2-4, sometimes with a second brood.

FEEDER BEHAVIOR: Does not visit feeders.

COMPARE TO SIMILAR SPECIES: Most similar to Black-billed Cuckoo, which has white tail spots that are only a third to half the size of the Yellow-billed's, and which lacks a partial yellow coloration of the bill. In south Florida, the Mangrove Cuckoo has a dark brown mask, a buffy cast to the belly, and yellow which is exclusively present on the lower half of the bill.

DID YOU KNOW? The Yellow-billed Cuckoo has a fascinating ocular adaptation that is well-suited to its relatively inactive, stealthy feeding habits. The eyes are positioned on either side of its head in such a way—combined with shallow sight-line indentations—as to allow the individual to see nearly 360 degrees without swiveling its head.

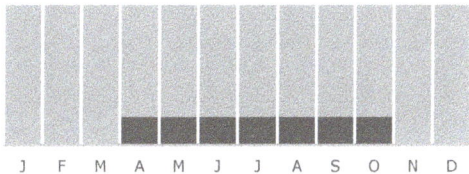

J F M A M J J A S O N D

② BLACK-BELLIED PLOVER (or GREY PLOVER).
Pluvialis squatarola.

SIZE: 11 in.

HABITAT: Beaches and tidal zones of shorelines; usually along oceanic coast at wintering grounds, and on very large lakes (e.g., Great Lakes) during migration. Sometimes, nearby wetlands and fields.

WILD DIET: Insects and small invertebrates (e.g., snails, crabs, worms).

BEHAVIOR: Standing and scurrying across the sand in near equal measure, this species tracks down potential prey items by sight. May be observed in large groups when high tide significantly decreases foraging space, though typically more widely dispersed.

MIGRATE? Partially.

NESTING: Breeds in the northernmost reaches of Canada and Alaska. Forms a shallow nest scrape, and lines this with loose vegetation and twigs. About 5 in. across.

EGGS: Light brown or light green-blue, with dark spotting and mottling. Length of 2 in. Total of 3-4.

FEEDER BEHAVIOR: Does not visit feeders.

COMPARE TO SIMILAR SPECIES: Most similar to the slightly smaller, more stubby-billed American Golden-Plover. During breeding season, note the dark gray cap on the head of the American Golden, as well as the lack of a white rear underside. During the nonbreeding months, American Golden has a far more defined white eyeline.

DID YOU KNOW? Overhunting of shorebirds decimated many species populations around the turn of the 20th Century, but the wariness of the Black-bellied Plover appeared to have saved it from the same fate. It is quite vigilant in its watch for predators, and other shorebirds sharing the same beaches have learned to recognize its vociferous, high-whistling alarm calls.

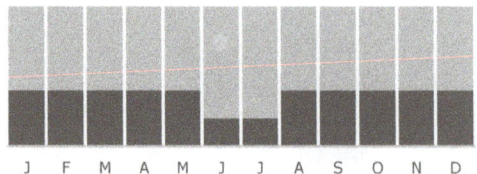

J F M A M J J A S O N D

Breeding adult at top (Photo by Hans Hillewaert / CC BY-SA / Cropped),
Nonbreeding adult at bottom.

Adults at top and bottom.

① MONK PARAKEET (or QUAKER PARAKEET).
Myiopsitta monachus.

SIZE: 11 in.
HABITAT: Open woods, cities, suburbs, and parks.
WILD DIET: Nuts, seeds, fruits, berries, flowers, flower buds, and grains.
BEHAVIOR: Usually found in large groups, foraging both in branches and on the ground. Nests are highly visible and a clear indicator of a feral breeding colony. Most populations are highly localized.
MIGRATE? No.
NESTING: Selects a location in a tree or on a utility pole. Forms a large, ball-like stick nest, in which all members of the colony both nest and roost. Individual chambers are formed for each unit of the colony within the nest. Up to 6 ft. from end to end, but more commonly 2-3 ft. across. Utilized for many years, and expands over time.
EGGS: White. Length of 1 in. Total of 5-10, occasionally with a second brood.

BIRD FEEDING TIPS

FEEDER DIET: Fruit, black-oil and hulled sunflower seeds, safflower seed, cracked corn, peanuts and peanut hearts, oats, millet, milo. **FEEDER TYPES**: Ground, platforms, hoppers. **FEEDER BEHAVIOR**: Only found at feeders in areas with established, nearby feral populations. Flocking behavior may quickly overwhelm feeder stations.

COMPARE TO SIMILAR SPECIES: Among parrots and parakeets, look for the pale upper chest and face of this species.

DID YOU KNOW? An invasive species originally native to central South America, releases from the pet trade have established wild populations across Florida and Texas, as well as in greater Chicago, New York City, Philadelphia, and New Orleans. Feral populations are also known to exist throughout Europe, the Middle East, and Southeast Asia.

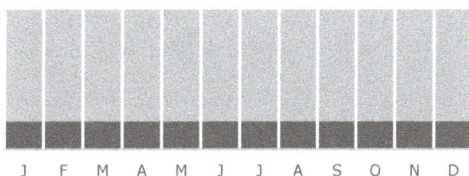

J F M A M J J A S O N D

(1) SHORT-BILLED DOWITCHER.
Limnodromus griseus.

SIZE: 11 in.

HABITAT: During migration, mudflats, wetlands, flooded fields, ponds, and lakes. When wintering, prefers saltwater or brackish tidal zones along the oceanic coast.

WILD DIET: Aquatic insects and insect larvae, aquatic invertebrates (e.g., snails, crabs).

BEHAVIOR: Prefers the muddy shallows, where it can easily probe the water for prey with the lower half of its bill. This species is well known for the back-and-forth motion of its bill in the substrate, rather like the needle of a sewing machine. Due to the tactility of its feeding and its superior low-light vision, dowitchers can often be found feeding after dark.

MIGRATE? No.

NESTING: Breeds on the southern edge of Canadian and Alaskan tundra. Selects a grassy location near dense vegetation. Cup-shaped, and constructed with dried vegetation. Less than 5-6 in. across.

EGGS: Light brown with dark mottling. Length of 1 ½ in. Total of 4.

FEEDER BEHAVIOR: Does not visit feeders.

COMPARE TO SIMILAR SPECIES: The Long-billed Dowitcher was considered to be conspecific with this species until the mid-20th Century; as such, the two species of North American dowitchers remain possibly the most difficult to separate of all birds mentioned in this guide. The supercilium, or eyebrow arch, of the Long-billed is nearly straight (as opposed to the more distinctly rounded arch of the Short-billed), and the end of the Long-billed's bill lacks the downward curve of the Short-billed. The Long-billed emits a high-pitched flight call of *kweek* or *pweek*, while the Short-billed has a lower, more bubbly *tu tu tu...* in flight.

DID YOU KNOW? Despite the *Long-billed* and *Short-billed* designations for the two dowitcher species, there is plenty of overlap between their known ranges of bill length and, as such, this is not the best indicator for identification.

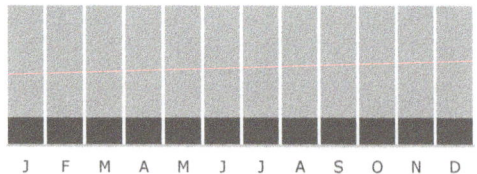

J F M A M J J A S O N D

Breeding adult at top (Photo by Dick Daniels / CC BY-SA / Cropped),
Nonbreeding Long-billed adult inset,
Nonbreeding adult at bottom (Photo by Dick Daniels / CC BY-SA).

Adults at top and bottom.

① **WILSON'S SNIPE.** *Gallinago delicata.*

SIZE: 11 in.
HABITAT: Wetlands, flooded fields, and ponds, usually with patches of dense vegetation.
WILD DIET: Insects and insect larvae, sometimes aquatic invertebrates.
BEHAVIOR: Pokes and probes its bill into mudflats and in shallow water while foraging. In part, this species is less commonly observed due to its camouflaging markings and penchant for concealing itself amid fallen logs and patches of vegetation. Sizable chest muscles allow for powerful wing strokes, which allow this rather portly bird to reach airspeeds of up to 65 mph—frequently resulting in a distinctive buzzing or winnowing sound from its feathers.
MIGRATE? Yes.
NESTING: Selects a concealed location adjacent to wetland shallows. A bowl-like impression is made in the soil or mud, and lined with woven reeds. About 6 in. across.
EGGS: Yellow-brown to creamy brown, with dark, cloudy mottling. Length of 1 ½ in. Total of 3-4.
FEEDER BEHAVIOR: Does not visit feeders.

COMPARE TO SIMILAR SPECIES: Solid brown stripe above pale eyeline on head, bold and dark patterning across body, and squat stature help to separate this species from the American Woodcock, which has a golden chest and different facial markings. Other similar species include the taller, leaner, less boldly patterned dowitchers (which sweep their bills back and forth while feeding).

DID YOU KNOW? This species is named for the early-1800s Scottish-American ornithologist Alexander Wilson, for whom the following species are also named: Wilson's Warbler, Wilson's Storm-Petrel, and Wilson's Phalarope. Wilson, along with his notable contemporary John James Audubon, was among the principal founders of the study of ornithology in North America.

J F M A M J J A S O N D

② BROWN THRASHER. *Toxostoma rufum.*

SIZE: 11 in.

HABITAT: Thickets, edges of woods.

WILD DIET: Mostly insects and spiders; also berries, nuts, and seeds.

BEHAVIOR: These fierce, boldly patterned birds are typically hidden in areas of dense vegetation, scrub, or overgrown thickets. Though this species may occasionally pick berries and nuts from bushes and trees, it is primarily seen foraging on the ground and in leaf litter with a deft sweeping motion of its decurved bill. Well known for its mimicry of a diverse array of sounds. During breeding season, males often claim a territory of up to several acres in size, which may reduce thrasher concentrations in some areas.

MIGRATE? Partially.

NESTING: Usually low in a protective shrub or tree. Cup-shaped, and constructed with twigs and sticks, as well as other vegetative matter. About 6 in. across.

EGGS: Light brown, blue, or blue-green, with fine brown speckling. Length of 1 in. Total of 2-5. Raises 1-3 broods each year, but usually 2.

BIRD FEEDING TIPS

FEEDER DIET: Black-oil and hulled sunflower seeds, suet, cracked corn, peanut hearts. **FEEDER TYPES**: Ground, platforms. **FEEDER BEHAVIOR**: Seldom visits backyards, given its preference for dense shrub cover, but may sift through fallen seeds and suet crumbs on the ground beneath feeders.

COMPARE TO SIMILAR SPECIES: Larger, with much longer tail, than Wood Thrush. Patterning, long and decurved bill, and long tail otherwise distinct.

DID YOU KNOW? Thrashers pugnaciously defend their nests, even to the point of drawing blood from dogs and humans.

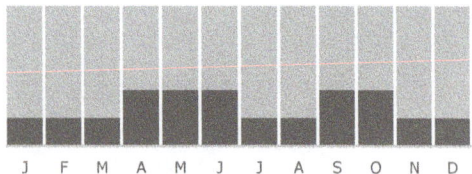

J F M A M J J A S O N D

Adults at top and bottom.

Adults at top and bottom.

⑤ **BLUE JAY.** *Cyanocitta cristata.*

SIZE: 11 in.

HABITAT: Any type of woods, but especially open woods and edges. Also common in all variety of wooded urban and suburban areas.

WILD DIET: Insects and spiders, nuts, grains, and seeds. May scavenge nearly anything else.

BEHAVIOR: Among the most visible of suburban birds, this species is noisy, active, and brightly colored. Jays are relatives of crows and ravens, and consequently possess many highly intelligent traits, such as intricate structuring of social systems, food caching, and accurate mimicry of other birds and animals. The raucous *jeer* of this species may carry for hundreds of yards across quiet sections of habitat.

MIGRATE? No.

NESTING: Selects a location amid the thick branches of a tree, about 10-20 ft. above the ground. Cup-shaped, constructed with soft twigs and grasses, and lined with plant roots. About 6-8 in. across, sometimes sprawling larger.

EGGS: Shades of blue to blue-green, with dirty mottling. Length of 1 in. Total of 3-6, sometimes with a second brood.

BIRD FEEDING TIPS

FEEDER DIET: Black-oil and hulled sunflower seeds, suet, safflower seed, mealworms, cracked corn, peanuts and peanut hearts, fruit, millet, milo. **FEEDER TYPES:** Platforms, suet cages, ground, hoppers, tubes. **FEEDER BEHAVIOR:** May yield to other birds when feeder is contested. Does not usually stay for long, unless very familiar with the surroundings.

COMPARE TO SIMILAR SPECIES: Distinct color and patterning for its size.

DID YOU KNOW? Blue Jays often push acorns into the ground during the fall months, saving them for colder days ahead. In fact, it is believed that this habit helped oak trees to recolonize much of North America following the last ice age.

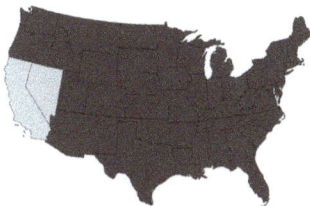

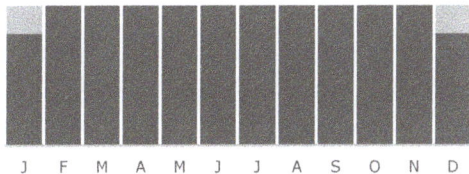

J F M A M J J A S O N D

179

② AMERICAN KESTREL. *Falco sparverius.*

SIZE: 11 in.

HABITAT: Open fields, including rural farmland and overgrown pasture. Occasionally, cities and suburbs.

WILD DIET: Insects (e.g., grasshoppers), small rodents (e.g., voles, mice) and birds, reptiles, and amphibians.

BEHAVIOR: Often observed scanning the ground from a perch, which may be a wire, post, fence, or exposed tree branch. It quickly dives or hovers as it approaches prey, which is usually struck directly on the ground. Upon returning to a perch, the kestrel consumes its prey piecemeal while holding it securely with one talon. Over a dozen catches may be made in a single hour, depending on the size and variety of prey targeted. Fastidious birders may also notice that individual kestrels tend to perfect their own hunting habits and techniques, similar to the behavior sometimes exhibited by the Peregrine Falcon, its much larger relative.

MIGRATE? Partially.

NESTING: Nests in various cavities, which may be old woodpecker hollows, rock crevices, or nooks in corners of buildings. No nest materials are used.

EGGS: Light brown or off-white, with dirty mottling. Length of 1 ½ in. Total of 3-6, occasionally with a second brood.

FEEDER BEHAVIOR: Rarely hunts at feeders.

COMPARE TO SIMILAR SPECIES: Though the size of a Mourning Dove, this species has bright, colorful markings (especially on males, which feature a bright orange chest and upper back) and a distinctive face. These facial markings, as well as their narrow, pointed wings in flight (characteristic of falcons, such as the Peregrine), help to differentiate from the Sharp-shinned Hawk.

DID YOU KNOW? The American Kestrel is the smallest of all North American falconids, and is hunted by all manner of larger falcons, owls, and hawks, even including the diminutive Sharp-shinned Hawk on occasion.

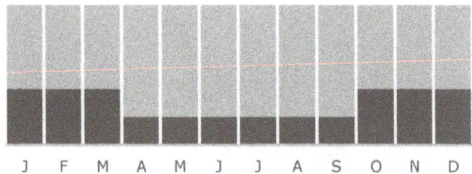

J F M A M J J A S O N D

Male at top (Photo by Greg Hume / CC BY-SA / Cropped),
Female at bottom (Photo by Andrew Dimler / CC BY-SA / Cropped).

Adult at top,
Juvenile at bottom (Photo by K6ka / CC BY-SA / Cropped).

③ AMERICAN ROBIN. *Turdus migratorius.*

SIZE: 10 in.
HABITAT: Open woods, parks, suburbs.
WILD DIET: Insects and spiders, worms, berries, and fruits.
BEHAVIOR: Often seen on suburban lawns, darting and pausing as it passes through the grass, and pulling worms from the soil. Particularly active immediately after rainfall (when worms move to the surface) or lawn mowing. Sings its undulating, cheery melodies of chirps for long periods while perched in trees. During colder months, may flock in very large groups to cooperatively search for food sources.
MIGRATE? Yes.
NESTING: Finds a location with ample leaf cover or protection, typically in trees or in artificial structures such as gutters, eaves, or streetlights. Cup-shaped, and composed of twigs and vegetation. About 6 in. across and 4 in. deep.
EGGS: Bright, light blue. Length of 1 in. Total of 3-5. Usually raises 2 broods each year, but may raise up to 3.

BIRD FEEDING TIPS

FEEDER DIET: Hulled sunflower seeds, suet, safflower seed, mealworms, fruit, peanut hearts. **FEEDER TYPES**: Ground, platforms. **FEEDER BEHAVIOR**: Very rarely visits feeders, but is frequently observable trotting through nearby lawns, gardens, and mulch beds.

COMPARE TO SIMILAR SPECIES: Juvenile could be confused with a Wood Thrush, but orange on chest and dark-colored head remain distinctive. Adults are quite distinctive and familiar.

DID YOU KNOW? The song of the American Robin has long been associated with the coming of spring, at which time males begin to vociferously seek out mates and defend their breeding territories. Emily Dickinson was especially fond of using this species as an allusion to springtime, with her poems ""Hope" is the thing with feathers" and "I dreaded that first robin so" serving as notable examples.

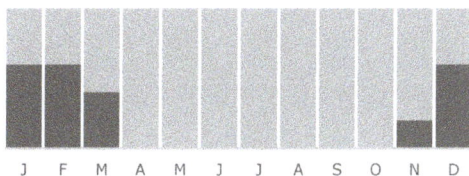

J F M A M J J A S O N D

183

(5) **RED-BELLIED WOODPECKER.**
Melanerpes carolinus.

SIZE: 9 ¾ in.

HABITAT: Various woods, wooded suburbs.

WILD DIET: Insects and spiders, seeds, nuts, fruits and berries.

BEHAVIOR: Like most woodpeckers, this species hops up and down tree trunks in search of food hidden beneath and between pieces of bark, using its sturdily built tail as a brace to facilitate such movements. Individuals are usually observed in a right-side-up position: inspecting, hammering, and then quickly grabbing food with the tongue. Individuals also frequently cache food in knots or crevices of trees.

MIGRATE? No.

NESTING: May select the trunk of a dead tree used in past years, but excavates a new nest cavity each year. Forms an entrance hole about 4 in. across, and a cavity 1 ft. deep.

EGGS: Shades of white. Length of 1 in. Total of 3-5. Usually raises 1-2 broods each year, but occasionally attempts to hatch and raise a third.

BIRD FEEDING TIPS

FEEDER DIET: Suet, black-oil and hulled sunflower seeds, peanuts and peanut hearts, safflower seed, cracked corn, grape jelly, mealworms, fruit, sugar water. **FEEDER TYPES**: Suet cages, tubes, hoppers, platforms, nectar feeders. **FEEDER BEHAVIOR**: Readily takes suet like many other woodpeckers, though may be present at other feeders as well. May assert its dominance and force other birds to scatter when it lands on a feeder.

COMPARE TO SIMILAR SPECIES: Individuals are often confused with Red-headed Woodpeckers, which possess an entirely red head and neck, rather than just a patch on top. Compared to the Northern Flicker, this species is slightly smaller and has different markings and coloration.

DID YOU KNOW? Due to its preference for building a nest cavity in dead trees, the Red-bellied Woodpecker is particularly vulnerable to the clearing of established woodlots and dying stands of forest.

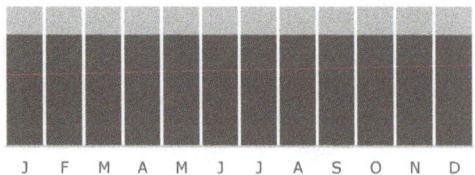

J F M A M J J A S O N D

Adult male feeding (Note that females have a red patch which extends only partway
up the back of the neck, and juveniles often have gray coloration on part or all of patch).

Adult at top,
Juvenile at bottom.

⑤ NORTHERN MOCKINGBIRD.
Mimus polyglottos.

SIZE: 9 ½ in.

HABITAT: Thickets, suburbs, and parks.

WILD DIET: Insects and spiders, worms, fruits (especially berries), and seeds.

BEHAVIOR: This species actively forages for food on the ground with erratic trots and pauses, as well as in shrubbery and in trees. It is perhaps best known for its diverse repertoire of songs, including detailed mimicries of other birds and neighborhood sounds alike. When singing, this species often sits on a high, elevated perch—such as a tree branch, pole, or fence post—and may continue its noisy vocalizations well into the nighttime hours, particularly during the warmer months. Northern Mockingbirds are also known to be among the most aggressive of all birds in the defense of their nests.

MIGRATE? No.

NESTING: Often nests around shoulder-height in trees and shrubs. Cup-shaped, composed mostly of twigs and vegetation. About 6 in. across.

EGGS: Light blue to blue-green, with brown splotches. Length of 1 in. Total of 3-5, with 2-3 broods.

BIRD FEEDING TIPS

FEEDER DIET: Fruit, mealworms, grape jelly, suet, hulled sunflower seeds, peanut hearts.
FEEDER TYPES: Ground, platforms. **FEEDER BEHAVIOR:** Uncommonly visits feeders, but may be attracted by (preferably, dense) plantings of native berry bushes.

COMPARE TO SIMILAR SPECIES: Much larger than Gray Catbird, and also differs in the following ways: paler in color, with a light underside; has bars of white on the wings; tail is more spread and feathered; and lacks a dark-colored patch atop the head.

DID YOU KNOW? This species was not historically present in large numbers north of Pennsylvania. However, the recent proliferation of multiflora rose has helped this mockingbird species expand its range northward. This decorative bush has white flowers, and is native to east Asia; consequently, it is an invasive species in North America and should not be actively planted in backyards.

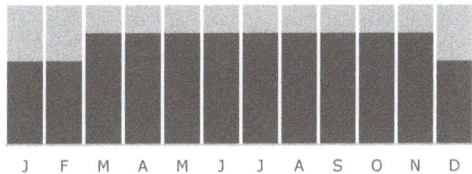

J   F   M   A   M   J   J   A   S   O   N   D

③ **KILLDEER.** *Charadrius vociferus.*

SIZE: 9 ½ in.

HABITAT: Fields, mudflats, wetlands, and beaches.

WILD DIET: Insects (e.g., beetles, flies), small aquatic invertebrates, worms.

BEHAVIOR: A plover of the ball fields, this species is one of the few shorebirds which regularly visits the rural suburbs. Often flocks when feeding, alternatingly running and pausing as each individual intently searches for food. When taking its invertebrate prey, the Killdeer either snaps up the item with its bill or yanks it forcefully from the substrate. Lone members of the flock aerially rove about nearby, seeking as-yet undiscovered feeding sites. Scatters quickly when approached. When flying, emits its characteristic, squeaky *kill-dee-ur* call.

MIGRATE? Partially.

NESTING: A shallow rut is scraped into the ground, upon which the eggs are laid. Close to 3 in. across.

EGGS: Whitish-tan, with many large black markings. Length of 1 ½ in. Total of 4-7. May raise 1-3 broods each year, but usually raises 2.

FEEDER BEHAVIOR: Does not visit feeders.

COMPARE TO SIMILAR SPECIES: Long, straight legs help to distinguish this as a shorebird; among other shorebirds and plovers, note this species' large size and two black chest rings (compared to the Semipalmated Plover's one).

DID YOU KNOW? During the breeding season, the Killdeer is well known for diverting predators' attention away from its nests by utilizing several notable display tactics. It may use "broken-wing" displays to lure a predator away before taking evasive flight, or alternatively spread its feathers and directly charge the intruder. However, it is best to watch from a safe distance: *never* closely approach bird nests, as this can adversely affect breeding success.

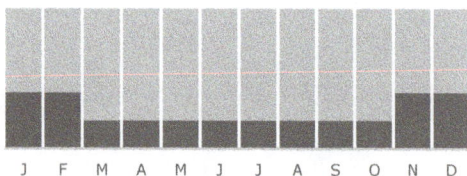

J F M A M J J A S O N D

Adult wading at top,
Adults in flight at bottom (Photo by Magnus Manske / CC BY-SA).

Adult roosting at top,
Adult feeding at dusk at bottom.

MEDIUM TO LARGE BIRDS (8 ½ - 12″)

② COMMON NIGHTHAWK. *Chordeiles minor.*

SIZE: 9 ¼ in.

HABITAT: Open country, including grasslands and open woods. Sometimes, cities.

WILD DIET: Flying insects (e.g., flies, moths, crickets).

BEHAVIOR: Active mostly at dawn and dusk, this species opens its mouth wide as it flies through scattered clouds of flying insects. Its winding flight path consists of darts, quick turns, and circling at heights which rarely exceed more than a few dozen feet; the nighthawk lightly flaps its aerodynamic wings to maintain speed as it irregularly dives near the ground. Often attracted to bright lights in parking lots or ballparks, where insects congregate in vast swarms. In overcast weather, may be occasionally observed flying and foraging during daylight hours.

MIGRATE? Yes.

NESTING: Directly on the ground, which may consist of soil, leaf litter, gravel, sand, or rocks. No rearrangement or addition of materials. In cities, may use flat roofs with a gravel covering.

EGGS: Off-white, with light speckling. Length of 1 in. Total of 2, occasionally with a second brood.

FEEDER BEHAVIOR: Does not visit feeders.

COMPARE TO SIMILAR SPECIES: Most other nightjars, with the exception of the nighthawks, have a larger relative head size and clearly rounded wingtips in flight. The slightly smaller Lesser Nighthawk is lighter and buffier overall, with white wing bars closer to the wingtips, and which are slightly less pronounced.

DID YOU KNOW? Nighthawks and nightjars are collectively known as goatsuckers, due to a mistaken former belief that these birds entered barns at night to suckle from goats; this notion was even quoted over two millennia ago by Aristotle.

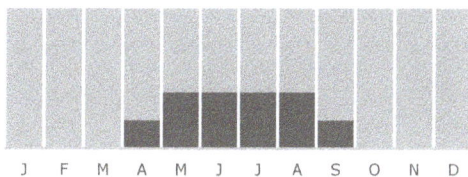

J F M A M J J A S O N D

① LEASTERN. *Sternula antillarum.*

SIZE: 9 in.

HABITAT: Breeds on coastlines of oceans and lakes, especially semi-sheltered bays and inlets; also, moves up rivers in the central U.S. Winters south of U.S.

WILD DIET: Small fish and crustaceans.

BEHAVIOR The smallest of the North American terns, this species is often conspicuous among seabirds for its diminutive size. Often observed scanning the water as it flies above; upon sighting a school of small fish, it typically plunges to the surface bill-first and quickly takes off with prey in tow, after minimal submersion. Least Terns are capable of quick, nimble flight as they weave and circle about their hunting grounds, navigating with brief flits of the wings.

MIGRATE? Yes.

NESTING: Loose colonial nester. Nest is located on beaches of shorelines or small islands, and consists of a shallow indentation in the substrate. About 6 in. across.

EGGS: Off-white, light brown, or blue, with dark mottling or spotting. Length of 1 in. Total of 1-4, occasionally with a second brood.

FEEDER BEHAVIOR: Does not visit feeders.

COMPARE TO SIMILAR SPECIES: Straight, pointed bill distinguishes from gulls, while size is far smaller than that of most other terns. The Black Tern is the only tern of similar size which shares territory with this species, but possesses conspicuous dark or black coloration throughout the body.

DID YOU KNOW? In the past half-century, Least Tern populations have decreased by 75 to 95%, with contributing factors including the following: domestic cats and dogs predating on their ground-based nests; increased human activity surrounding known breeding colonies; and threats to fish populations due to invasive species, pollutants, and industrial development.

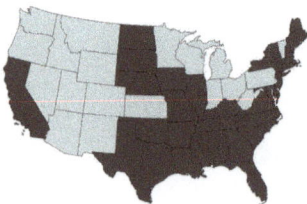

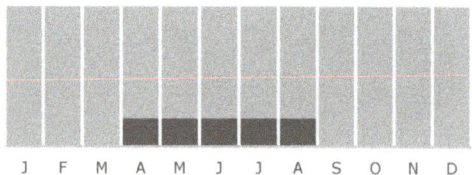

J F M A M J J A S O N D

Adults in breeding plumage at top and bottom (Note: Bill changes in color
to black in Sept., after breeding season has passed).

Adults at top and bottom.

② EASTERN MEADOWLARK. *Sturnella magna.*

SIZE: 9 in.

HABITAT: Somewhat thick fields, grasslands, and prairies.

WILD DIET: Mostly insects, but also seeds and grains (particularly in the winter).

BEHAVIOR: Best known for whistling its distinctive song from elevated perches during breeding season, but is usually less noticeable throughout the remainder of the year, especially in the North. While walking across the ground, forages by probing and prying apart the soil in search of a variety of insects; it accomplishes this feat with its considerably strong jaw muscles. Polygynous by nature, each male will defend a territory of two to three resident females, each with whom he will mate.

MIGRATE? No.

NESTING: Selects a small rut in the ground, and constructs nest on top. Cup-shaped, with stems and grasses used. About 8 in. across and 2 in. deep.

EGGS: White to light blue, with brown mottling. Length of 1 in. Total of 3-6, with 2 broods.

BIRD FEEDING TIPS

FEEDER DIET: Cracked corn, hulled sunflower seeds. **FEEDER TYPES**: Ground. **FEEDER BEHAVIOR**: Very uncommon at feeders. Visits are typically during wintertime, when insects are scarce.

COMPARE TO SIMILAR SPECIES: The Western Meadowlark is nearly identical to the Eastern, though their ranges only overlap in the western Midwest U.S. These species are best differentiated by song (Western has flute-like, more garbled two-phrase song, compared to Eastern's higher, clear, one-phrase whistles), though the former is also unreliably identified by the brown lines across its head, which are lighter. Also, this species is somewhat similar to the Dickcissel, but larger size, fully yellow belly, and longer bill are distinct to the meadowlarks.

DID YOU KNOW? While Western Meadowlarks sing about a dozen variations of their common melody, Easterns can have repertoires of over 100 different, but consistent, patterns—each of which still resembles the original song.

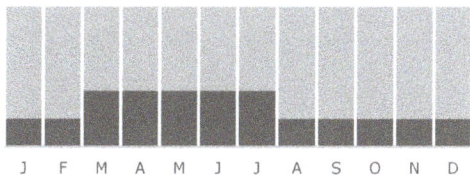

J F M A M J J A S O N D

⑤ NORTHERN CARDINAL. *Cardinalis cardinalis.*

SIZE: 8 ¾ in.

HABITAT: Open woods, cities and suburbs. Also, thickets and scrub.

WILD DIET: Seeds, fruits, and grains. Sometimes, insects.

BEHAVIOR: Conceivably the most photographed bird in North America, this species is often found perched in various shrubs, trees, and even in sheltered surroundings on the ground. Individuals typically stay at each foraging location for several minutes or longer. In late spring and summer, frequently sings from prominent, elevated perches to defend territory. Song is an ascending and whistled *wheet, wheet, ..., wheet*, followed immediately by a quick series of *chew, chew, ..., chew*. Also calls repeatedly with loud metallic chinks.

MIGRATE? No.

NESTING: Prefers locations with dense leaf cover, usually in a tree or shrub. Nest bowl is woven of twigs, and lined with finer grasses, stems. About 3-4 in. across.

EGGS: Off-white to light blue-green, with brown speckling or mottling. Length of 1 in. Total of 2-4, with 2-3 broods.

BIRD FEEDING TIPS

FEEDER DIET: Black-oil and hulled sunflower seeds, safflower seed, peanut hearts, cracked corn, millet, milo. **FEEDER TYPES**: Platforms, hoppers, tubes, ground. **FEEDER BEHAVIOR**: Very common visitor, and one of the first species to repeatedly visit new feeders. Often observed in male-female pairs, especially during spring and summer.

COMPARE TO SIMILAR SPECIES: Male Summer and Scarlet Tanagers are also bright red—particularly the former—but the Northern Cardinal is larger, has a black mask, and has a conspicuous head crest.

DID YOU KNOW? In May and June, cardinals are very territorial toward other individuals of the same species, periodically going so far as to attack their own reflections in windows or panes of glass. Other species—particularly those which nest in the suburbs, such as the American Robin—have also been known to occasionally engage in similar behaviors.

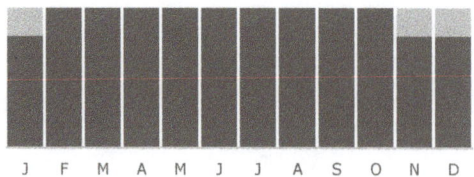

J F M A M J J A S O N D

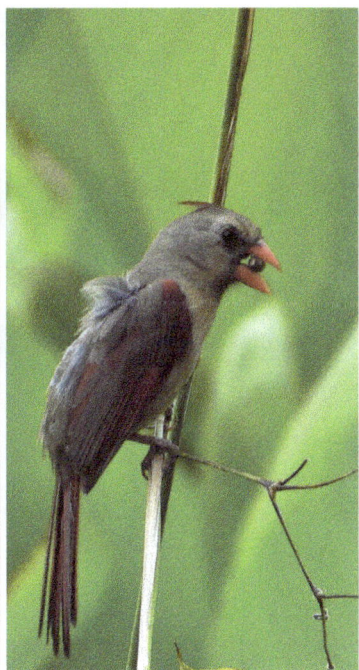

Adult male at top,
Adult female at bottom left,
Juvenile female at bottom right.

Adults at top and bottom.

④ **GRAY CATBIRD.** *Dumetella carolinensis.*

SIZE: 8 ¾ in.

HABITAT: Thickets, edges of woods, overgrown fields, cities and suburbs.

WILD DIET: Fruits and berries (e.g., holly berries, poison ivy), and insects.

BEHAVIOR: This species is ordinarily sequestered away in tangles of shrubs and vines, hopping about while gleaning fruits and berries from the branches or ground. Most easily recognizable due to its repeated, raspy mewing call—rather like that of a cantankerous feline.

MIGRATE? Yes.

NESTING: Concealed in dense shrub foliage. Bowl of twigs and dried grasses, and lined with softer materials, such as pine needles. About 5-6 in. across.

EGGS: Bright turquoise. Length of 1 in. Total of 1-5, with 2 broods.

BIRD FEEDING TIPS

FEEDER DIET: Mealworms, suet, grape jelly, fruit. **FEEDER TYPES**: Ground, platforms, suet cages. **FEEDER BEHAVIOR**: Uncommon visitor, but known to retrieve suet droppings from ground. Particularly in May and June, may also take mealworms and fruit from platforms.

COMPARE TO SIMILAR SPECIES: Most similar to the larger Northern Mockingbird, but note the Gray Catbird's distinct black head cap, lack of white barring on wings, and overall darker silhouette.

DID YOU KNOW? It is thought that most catbirds which nest along the Atlantic Seaboard winter in Florida or the Caribbean, with most Midwestern birds nesting in Central America. Once the winter is complete, the flocks return to the same local territories where they spent the previous summer—possibly even visiting the same backyards year after year.

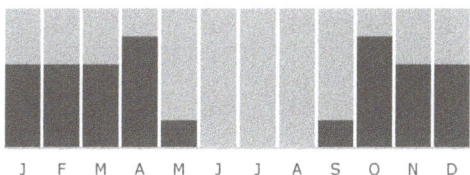

J F M A M J J A S O N D

② **LOGGERHEAD SHRIKE.** *Lanius ludovicianus.*

SIZE: 8 ¾ in.

HABITAT: Open woods and fields, preferably with short ground vegetation.

WILD DIET: Insects and spiders, small birds, reptiles and amphibians, rodents, and bats.

BEHAVIOR: Though this songbird mostly eats insects, it commonly—and infamously—is predatory toward vertebrates as well. In the strictest sense, shrikes are not birds of prey, as their talons are too weak to carry prey; individuals compensate for this by steeply diving from a perch to deliver maximum blunt-force trauma to the quarry, before dragging or flying away with the quarry for feeding. The prey is often butchered by impalement on a sharp thorn or branch, after which the shrike is able to turn its full attention to the task of tearing away bite-sized pieces with its bill. Individuals may return to impaled carcasses to more fully consume at a later date.

MIGRATE? Partially.

NESTING: Selects a location in dense, sometimes thorny bushes or trees. A platform with a central cup is constructed; this structure is woven of twigs, dried grasses, or roots, and lined with feathers and moss. Cup is about 5-6 in. across.

EGGS: Off-white, with light brown speckling. Length of 1 in. Total of 5-7, with 2 broods.

FEEDER BEHAVIOR: Does not normally visit feeders, but may perch nearby in hope of taking small songbirds, often from the ground.

COMPARE TO SIMILAR SPECIES: Similar to the larger Northern Shrike, but Loggerheads have a broader black mask without prominent white markings above the eye and mask. Loggerhead also has a blunter bill, without the protrusive hook of the Northern.

DID YOU KNOW? Though this species was formerly native to the entirety of the contiguous U.S. and southern Canada, it is now found nearly exclusively in more southerly latitudes—with the species now listed by some organizations as critically endangered in Canada.

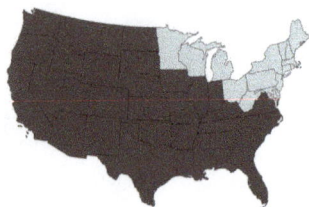

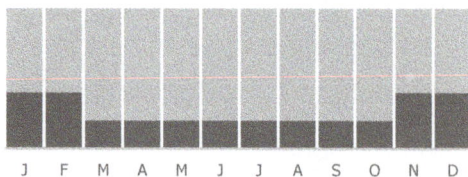

J F M A M J J A S O N D

Adults at top and bottom.

Adult at top,
Juvenile at bottom.

① RED-HEADED WOODPECKER.
Melanerpes erythrocephalus.

SIZE: 8 ¾ in.

HABITAT: Open woods and groves, suburbs, and wooded sections of cities.

WILD DIET: Nuts, insects, fruits, and seeds.

BEHAVIOR: Forages in trees—occasionally on the ground—for nuts, fruits, and seeds. Known to catch flying insects with quick flights reminiscent of flycatchers. Often stores food, including trapped live insects, in small spaces under sections of bark or roof shingles; this species is the only woodpecker which is known to cache food in this secretive manner. Flight path is less undulating than that of other woodpeckers, often moving with a more or less continuous, straight path.

MIGRATE? No.

NESTING: Drills a cavity in a dead or dying tree, or sometimes a utility pole. Often reused in subsequent years. About 3 in. across and 1 ft. deep.

EGGS: Bright white. Length of 1 in. Total of 4-6, sometimes with a second brood.

BIRD FEEDING TIPS

FEEDER DIET: Suet, black-oil and hulled sunflower seeds, peanuts and peanut hearts, mealworms, safflower seed. **FEEDER TYPES**: Suet cages, tubes, hoppers, platforms. **FEEDER BEHAVIOR**: Uncommon across much of range, but known to visit locations with suet cages and seed bells, in particular. Rarely uses nest boxes.

COMPARE TO SIMILAR SPECIES: Adult's fully crimson head and neck are highly distinctive, along with bold black-and-white barring on back.

DID YOU KNOW? The specific name for this bird, *erythrocephalus*, can be easily dissected into its two constituent Greek roots: *erythro-*, or red; and *cephalus*, or head. In the annals of Greek mythology, Cephalus was the great-grandfather of Homer's Odysseus, thus making him the "head" of an exceptionally estimable family.

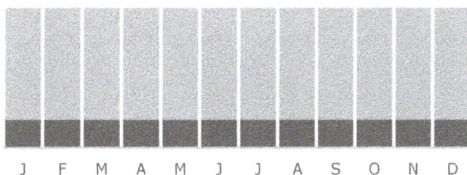

J F M A M J J A S O N D

④ EUROPEAN STARLING. *Sturnus vulgaris.*

SIZE: 8 ¼ in.

HABITAT: Cities and suburbs, agricultural fields. Often perched on power lines.

WILD DIET: Mostly insects (e.g., grasshoppers, flies) and spiders. Also, fruit and berries, seeds, grains, and garbage.

BEHAVIOR: This invasive species from Europe is most commonly observed in large, wheeling flocks of hundreds, or even thousands, which swarm across the sky—a flocking motion once described by the poet Dante Alighieri as seemingly being pushed by gusts of wind. These birds may forage in agricultural fields, on recently mowed lawns, or in urban centers, exhausting local resources before moving on. Calls include harsh chattering, buzzing, whistling, and rattling noises.

MIGRATE? No.

NESTING: Cavity nester. Selected cavities may include manmade openings (e.g., streetlights), former woodpecker nests, and nest boxes. A shallow bowl is formed inside, constructed of dried grasses. On average, about 8 in. wide.

EGGS: Light blue-green. Length of 1 in. Total of 4-6, with 2 broods.

BIRD FEEDING TIPS

FEEDER DIET: Black-oil and hulled sunflower seeds, suet, cracked corn, peanuts and peanut hearts, millet, oats, milo, fruit. **FEEDER TYPES:** Platforms, hoppers, tubes, ground, suet cages. **FEEDER BEHAVIOR:** Can quickly overrun feeders, a circumstance which can be averted by solely offering safflower seed at some stations. Also, may use nest boxes.

COMPARE TO SIMILAR SPECIES: Very distinctive appearance and profile, and rather unlike most other North American species.

DID YOU KNOW? About 100 starlings were originally introduced to Central Park in 1890 and 1891 by Shakespeare enthusiasts, in homage to a brief account of the species in *Henry IV*. In the years since, however, they have established themselves as one of the most abundant species continent-wide, which has led to the concomitant decline of many native cavity-nesting species, such as the Purple Martin.

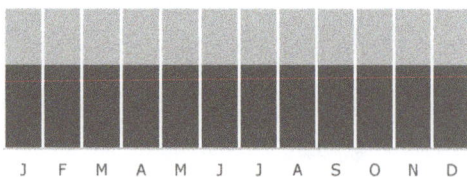

J F M A M J J A S O N D

Breeding adult at top (Jan. to Aug.),
Nonbreeding adult at bottom left (Sept. to Jan.),
Flock at bottom right (Photo by John Holmes / CC BY-SA / Cropped).

Adult male at top,
Adult female at bottom left,
Juvenile male at bottom right (Notice "in-between," dirty stage of coloration).

④ RED-WINGED BLACKBIRD.
Agelaius phoeniceus.

SIZE: 8 in.

HABITAT: Marshes and ponds, flooded fields, weedy fields. Sometimes along the median strip or roadsides of highways.

WILD DIET: Seeds and grains. In warmer months, half of diet also consists of insects.

BEHAVIOR: The archetypal wetland passerine, or perching bird, this species is known for inhabiting nearby dense tangles of brush and thicket. Opportunistically forages for insects whenever available, and otherwise is a prodigious consumer of seeds and grains. One of the most population-dense species in North America, due to the male's tendency to mate with and defend five to 15 females, and its highly aggressive nest-defense tactics. Song is *kok-a-reeee*, with particular emphasis and length placed on the final, slurred and trilled syllable. This rattling din is just about inescapable in wetter environs.

MIGRATE? No.

NESTING: Weaves a neat cup of grasses and reeds, often amid tall shoots of vegetation. About 6 in. across and 4 in. deep.

EGGS: Light turquoise, with dark markings. Length of 1 in. Total of 2-4. Raises 1-3 broods each year, usually 2.

BIRD FEEDING TIPS

FEEDER DIET: Black-oil and hulled sunflower seeds, cracked corn, suet, peanut hearts, oats, millet, milo. **FEEDER TYPES**: Suet cages, platforms, hoppers, tubes. **FEEDER BEHAVIOR**: Most likely to visit in late fall to mid-spring, when insects are less plentiful.

COMPARE TO SIMILAR SPECIES: Male's red-orange wing patch is highly distinctive; female is much smaller and more sparrow-like, but notice her sharp, pointed bill, as well as the defined, light eyeline.

DID YOU KNOW? Males with larger red wing patches are more aggressive and better at defending their territories from rivals. This likely serves as a biological signaling mechanism, and is produced by dietary carotenoid pigments; in fact, this same class of pigments gives carrots their familiar orange hue.

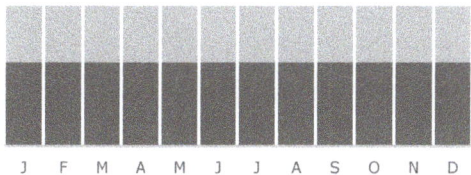

J F M A M J J A S O N D

② EASTERN TOWHEE. *Pipilo erythrophthalmus.*

SIZE: 8 in.

HABITAT: Mostly thickets—in open woods, overgrown fields, and hedgerows.

WILD DIET: Seeds, fruits, buds, insects and spiders, and snails.

BEHAVIOR: This oversized sparrow moves slowly, but noisily, through understories of woods and overgrown fields. Over three-quarters of foraging is conducted on the ground, with occasional forays onto low branches. Prefers to strip away leaf litter to uncover potential food items, often using a characteristic two-legged, backward scratch-and-hop motion. Given the dense cover of its typical habitat, this species is more often seen than heard. Its song resembles *drink-your-teeeeaaaa*, with the final syllable high and trilled; the call is a squeaky, yanking, and ascending *chewink*.

MIGRATE? Yes.

NESTING: Selects a concealed location on the ground, with the nest sunken into leaf litter amid surrounding vegetation. Finely woven bowl of twigs, grasses, and stems. About 4-5 in. across.

EGGS: Off-white or light pink, with dense, light brown spotting. Length of 1 in. Total of 2-6. Raises 1-3 broods each year, usually 2.

BIRD FEEDING TIPS

FEEDER DIET: Black-oil and hulled sunflower seeds, cracked corn, peanut hearts, millet, milo. **FEEDER TYPES**: Ground, platforms. **FEEDER BEHAVIOR**: Most common in yards with dense shrubbery or hedgerows, particularly near woods with a thicketed understory. Animatedly scratches along the ground for seeds.

COMPARE TO SIMILAR SPECIES: Spotted Towhee of the Great Plains is similar, but has extensive white spotting along the wing. In addition, American Robin also has orange on underside, but Eastern Towhee has a bright white belly.

DID YOU KNOW? The towhee's common name is onomatopoeic, specifically relating to its *towhee* call, which is more often described as a *chewink* (*See* Behavior).

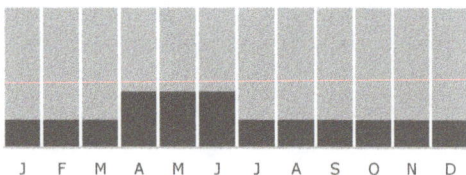

J F M A M J J A S O N D

Adult male performing a scratch-and-hop at top,
Adult female at bottom (Photo by Shawn Taylor / CC BY-SA / Cropped).

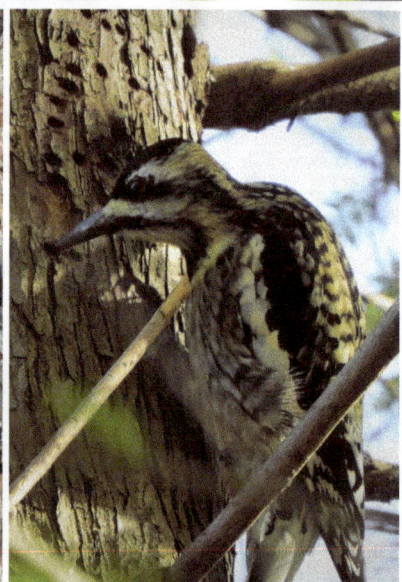

Adult female at top (Notice white throat),
Adult male at bottom left (Notice red throat),
Juvenile at bottom right.

① YELLOW-BELLIED SAPSUCKER.
Sphyrapicus varius.

SIZE: 8 in.

HABITAT: Dense to semi-open woods. Often favors woods with plenty of younger, faster-growing trees. Sometimes, orchards.

WILD DIET: Sap, insects (e.g., carpenter ants) and spiders. Sometimes, fruit.

BEHAVIOR: This species drills neat rows of shallow, narrow wells into the inner tissue of tree trunks. These wells are constantly maintained to keep the sap flowing, and further rows are drilled in productive trees to form ordered, dotlike grids. Trees which are frequently used include maples, birches, hickories, and poplars. May also feed on flying insects, and any ants attracted to their sap wells. Idiosyncratic drumming pattern is erratic, and sounds rather like the transmission of an esoteric Morse code message.

MIGRATE? Yes.

NESTING: Excavates a cavity in a dying or decaying tree. Entrance is less than 2 in. across, and nest hole is approximately 9 in. deep.

EGGS: White. Length of 1 in. Total of 4-7.

BIRD FEEDING TIPS

FEEDER DIET: Grape jelly, suet, sugar water, mealworms. **FEEDER TYPES**: Suet cages, platforms, nectar feeders. **FEEDER BEHAVIOR**: Uncommon visitor, but may be regularly attracted by small cups of grape jelly or sugar water, as well as by suet cages.

COMPARE TO SIMILAR SPECIES: Head patterning is particularly distinctive.

DID YOU KNOW? Other species actively benefit from the prolific drilling of sapsuckers, including the porcupines, squirrels, nuthatches, and bats which readily take advantage of the accompanying gratis food source. In addition, hummingbirds have even been known to time spring migrations in line with those of sapsuckers, with breeding success increased by the local presence of open sap wells.

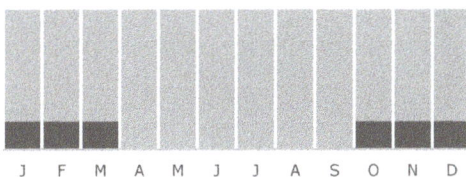

J F M A M J J A S O N D

② **PURPLE MARTIN.** *Progne subis.*

SIZE: 7 ¾ in.

HABITAT: Cities and suburbs, likely near established martin houses. Often prefers open areas, especially near sources of water.

WILD DIET: Flying insects (e.g., dragonflies, butterflies, grasshoppers, ants).

BEHAVIOR: Circles high in the air, often at heights of 100 to 200 feet, while hunting insects on the wing. Flying motion consists of a quick series of flaps, followed by long, graceful glides. Often found in very large groups, both near established colonies and when roosting in late summer.

MIGRATE? Yes.

NESTING: Colonial cavity nester. Mostly uses martin houses now (*See* Feeder Behavior) due to the omnipresence of invasive European Starlings and House Sparrows, which also use natural cavities. A ragged bowl of twigs is assembled inside the cavity, and is sometimes lined with leaves. About 8 in. across.

EGGS: White. Length of 1 in. Total of 3-6.

FEEDER BEHAVIOR: Does not visit feeders, but does use specially designed martin houses. These elevated birdhouses are painted white and typically consist of multiple compartments, are placed on a pole at a height of 10-18 feet, and are situated in relatively open fields, particularly near water. Some setups also use groupings of gourd-like bulbs. It is crucial to use starling-resistant entrance holes, and to safeguard against ground predators. Individual compartments should be about 8 in. across and 12 in. deep.

COMPARE TO SIMILAR SPECIES: May be confused with similarly sized European Starling, but note the Purple Martin's forked tail, backswept wings, and aerial hawking behavior. Compared to other swallows (which are generally much smaller), male is the only dark-bellied bird, and the female has a dirty, streaked underside.

DID YOU KNOW? Even before the European colonization of the Americas, the Native Americans were known to hang empty gourds for nesting Purple Martins.

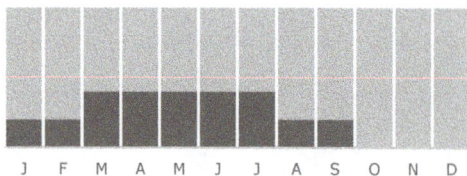

J F M A M J J A S O N D

Male at top,
Female with male at bottom (Photo by Sam May / CC BY-SA / Cropped).

Adult male at top,
Adult female at bottom (Note: Juveniles are slightly drabber, buffier by comparison).

① **BALTIMORE ORIOLE.** *Icterus galbula.*

SIZE: 7 ¾ in.
HABITAT: Open woods, suburbs, parks, and orchards.
WILD DIET: Berries and fruits, insects, and nectar.
BEHAVIOR: Best known for its penchant for gleaning berries and fruits from trees and bushes all across its territory, this species actually takes more insects than fruits during the breeding season—in keeping with the young's higher protein needs. Busily clambers and clings from all angles as it forages for such items as caterpillars, mulberries, and grapes. When feeding on larger fruits, punctures the surface with its bill, before opening and slurping with deft strokes of its brushlike tongue. In springtime, particularly well-known for its chattering, flute-like whistles.
MIGRATE? Yes.
NESTING: In the upper reaches of a tree, weaves a hanging, bindle-like nest of fine grasses and hairs: a marvel of construction. About 4 in. across and 5 in. deep.
EGGS: Off-white to blue-green, with dark streaking and splotches. Length of 1 in. Total of 3-6.

BIRD FEEDING TIPS

FEEDER DIET: Fruit, grape jelly, sugar water, suet. **FEEDER TYPES**: Platforms, nectar feeders. **FEEDER BEHAVIOR**: Prefers to take orange slices and grape jelly from small platform cups. Also visits nectar feeders. Ceteris paribus, usually attracted to the color orange. More likely to visit feeders outside of breeding season.

COMPARE TO SIMILAR SPECIES: Among males, bright orange underside (compared to smaller Orchard Oriole's dark orange) and full black head and neck are diagnostic. Females have washed-out, yellow-orange coloration on the chest and belly—the only oriole dames with a fully orange-hued underside—and a dirty head and back.

DID YOU KNOW? Despite its fiery plumage, this species is actually a member of the blackbird, or icterid, family.

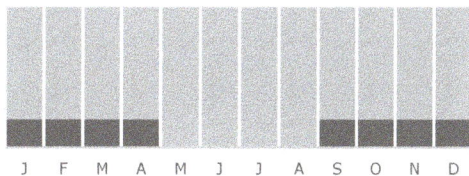

J F M A M J J A S O N D

③ BROWN-HEADED COWBIRD. *Molothrus ater.*

SIZE: 7 ½ in.

HABITAT: Edges of woods, open fields, suburbs.

WILD DIET: Seeds, grains, insects. Sometimes eggs of other birds.

BEHAVIOR: Often announces its presence with a short, liquid-like chortle, immediately followed by a thin, high whistle. Customarily forages on the ground, and may also be found perching in trees and bushes. In fields, known to snap up insects disturbed by grazing livestock. Males and females both practice promiscuous mating, with few seasonally established pairs. Juveniles hatch sooner than the young of their host nests (*See* Nesting), and mature much more rapidly; this allows the young cowbird to monopolize resources and frequently outcompete the other members of its cohort.

MIGRATE? No.

NESTING: Brood parasite: lays eggs in nests of other birds, usually smaller species (e.g., sparrows, warblers).

EGGS: Off-white, with dense brown speckling. Length of 1 in. Total of 1-4 per nest, with up to 40 eggs per season.

BIRD FEEDING TIPS

FEEDER DIET: Black-oil and hulled sunflower seeds, cracked corn, peanut hearts, suet, millet, oats, milo. **FEEDER TYPES**: Ground, platforms, hoppers, tubes, suet cages. **FEEDER BEHAVIOR**: A highly opportunistic forager, this species is a partisan of feeder setups of nearly all varieties, and may also congregate on the ground for spilled feed. From May to July, juveniles are often observed following adoptive mothers of other species.

COMPARE TO SIMILAR SPECIES: Notice male's distinctive brown head and neck; females and juveniles are duller brown and sparrow-like, but are drabber and lack extensive, well-defined streaking. Also, notice this species' characteristically stout bill, another useful field mark.

DID YOU KNOW? It is thought that the Brown-headed Cowbird's parasitic nesting behavior originally evolved due to necessity, having previously subsisted by following grazing bison across the Great Plains. As it was never in one location for more than a few weeks, it was thus not able to incubate its own young—relying on other species for this task. However, with the fragmentation of woodland due to human development (and the consequent creation of new fringe habitat), this species' further proliferation has seriously threatened populations of many woodland songbirds.

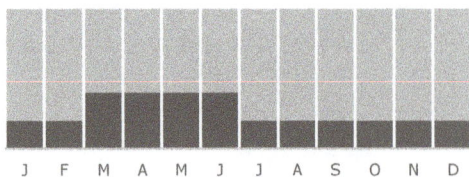

J F M A M J J A S O N D

Adult male at top,
Adult female at bottom,
Juveniles taking food from adoptive Common Yellowthroat mother, inset.

Breeding adult at top,
Chick climbing over a stone at bottom left,
Nonbreeding adult at bottom right.

② SPOTTED SANDPIPER. *Actitis macularius.*

SIZE: 7 ½ in.

HABITAT: Edges of rivers, ponds, and streams. Also, coastlines of oceans, lakes, and reservoirs. Seems to prefer rockier shorelines.

WILD DIET: Mostly insects and insect larvae. Also, small aquatic invertebrates.

BEHAVIOR: Steadily bobs its rear half as it goes about its day, a highly manifest and diagnostic behavior for this species. Often walks in seemingly undeliberate paths near the edge of the water or over rocks—until a quick pecking motion toward prey betrays the earnestness of its original intention. May take insects from the water surface, or even from midair. Usually found by itself or in small groups, though it is likely the most common North American sandpiper, particularly inland.

MIGRATE? Yes.

NESTING: In the vicinity of the water's edge, often tucked away beneath shrubs. May be situated near Common Tern colonies in some locations. A bowl-like scrape is made in the dirt, and lined with leaves and grasses. About 4 in. across.

EGGS: Off-white with brown mottling. Length of 1 - 1 ½ in. Total of 4, sometimes with a second brood.

FEEDER BEHAVIOR: Does not visit feeders.

COMPARE TO SIMILAR SPECIES: Polka-dot pattern on chest during breeding season is very distinctive among shorebirds. In nonbreeding plumage, look for its plain brown back and sides, as well as a white belly and the accompanying white coloration which rises along the sides of its breast.

DID YOU KNOW? Spotted Sandpipers are often polyandrous breeders. In this pattern, females take several mates, laying nests for each individual male to rear. Sequential polyandry of this nature is a rare breeding practice, and limited to just a few shorebird species, of which the Spotted Sandpiper is by far the most common.

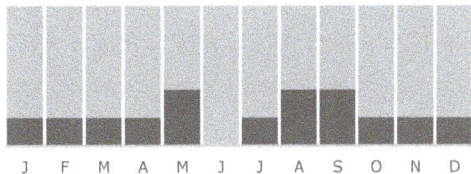

J F M A M J J A S O N D

③ **GREAT CRESTED FLYCATCHER.**
Myiarchus crinitus.

SIZE: 7 ½ in.

HABITAT: Mature, open to semi-open woods; forest clearings.

WILD DIET: Insects (e.g., butterflies, wasps, crickets). Occasionally, small fruits.

BEHAVIOR: Perches and flies high amid the treetops, exploiting a relatively unique ecological niche among the flycatchers. Individuals sally out for insect prey for longer periods of time, and are resultantly much less likely than other flycatchers to return to the same perch. Like many flycatchers, can be entertaining to watch in flight, as it darts and swoops in close pursuit of its prey. Sometimes observed nodding its head while perched, and singing with a variety of buzzing, ascending, *breep*-like whistles.

MIGRATE? Partially.

NESTING: Cavity nester. May use natural tree hollows, former woodpecker nests, and nesting boxes. Prefers hole with a depth of 5-8 in. Inside, constructs a loosely hewn bowl of grasses, twigs, and various debris. Bowl is about 3 in. across.

EGGS: Off-white to pink, with extensive dark red-brown splotching. Length of ¾ in. Total of 4-7.

FEEDER BEHAVIOR: Does not visit feeders, but does use nest boxes.

COMPARE TO SIMILAR SPECIES: Yellow belly, conspicuous crest, and rufous tail distinguish from other flycatchers.

DID YOU KNOW? This species is known to weave molted snakeskins into its nests whenever possible, particularly in regions where there are more prolific snake populations, such as in Georgia, Louisiana, and Florida. Some titmice also practice this behavior, which may attempt to discourage ovivorous (or egg-eating) trespassers from frequenting the nest.

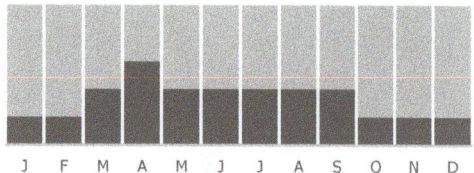

J F M A M J J A S O N D

Adults at top and bottom.

Male at top,
Female at bottom left,
Juvenile at bottom right.

③ EASTERN BLUEBIRD. *Sialia sialis.*

SIZE: 7 ¼ in.

HABITAT: Open country with some trees, including the following locations: rural fields, parks, golf courses, roadsides, orchards, open woods, and suburbs.

WILD DIET: Insects (e.g., grasshoppers, crickets), fruit and berries.

BEHAVIOR: Bluebirds are often found on lone or exposed perches (e.g., power lines, sign posts, tree branches), scanning the ground for insects. Once a movement has been recognized, the individual swoops to the ground, quickly takes the insect, and returns to a perch. Bluebirds may also glean fruits and berries in fall and winter, when insects are far less plentiful. A mildly varied repertoire of songs and calls includes sweet, warbling whistles and quick, raspy chattering.

MIGRATE? No.

NESTING: Cavity nester. Uses natural tree hollows, former woodpecker nests, and nest boxes. A plain, cramped bowl of dried grasses is woven and pressed together. Cavity is about 4-6 in. wide, with an entrance under 2 in. in diameter.

EGGS: Light blue-green. Length of ¾ in. Total of 3-7. Usually raises 2 broods each year, sometimes attempting to hatch and raise a third.

BIRD FEEDING TIPS

FEEDER DIET: Mealworms, fruit, suet, peanut hearts, black-oil and hulled sunflower seeds. **FEEDER TYPES:** Platforms, tubes, ground. **FEEDER BEHAVIOR:** May gather in small flocks, particularly if live mealworms are offered. Visits yards with native berry bushes in colder months. Also, uses manmade nest boxes (*See* Nesting).

COMPARE TO SIMILAR SPECIES: Somewhat similar to the Mountain Bluebird of the Rockies, but Eastern is the only resident bluebird with an orange wash on its breast. The smaller Tufted Titmouse has a conspicuous head crest, and a greyish back and tail.

DID YOU KNOW? The Eastern Bluebird's vision is well suited to its perch-and-pursuit hunting strategy, with individuals able to spot insects from over 25 yards.

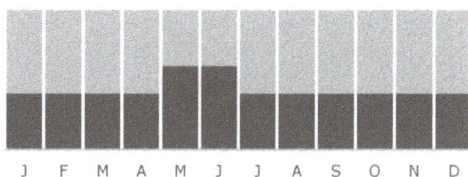

J F M A M J J A S O N D

③ **BARN SWALLOW.** *Hirundo rustica.*

SIZE: 7 in.

HABITAT: Various open fields (both suburban and rural), and over wetlands and lakes.

WILD DIET: Flying insects (e.g., flies, butterflies, aphids).

BEHAVIOR: Flies somewhat low over open country or water, snapping up large flying insects with its cavernous mouth. Wingbeats are quick, agile, and moderately shallow. Flocks are known to follow large machinery or livestock to feed on the insects disturbed by the activity. When flying over water, frequently dips to the surface, drinking and bathing while on the wing. Cheerfully jabbers while flying, often making *cheep* or *chureep* calls.

MIGRATE? Yes.

NESTING: Previously nested in caves, but now nests almost exclusively in barns and similar, artificial structures. Nest is a mud-and-grass mixture; this dries into a relatively firm cup, which is affixed to a vertical wall or horizontal beam. May be reused in future years. About 5-8 in. across.

EGGS: Off-white or light pink, with dark brown spotting. Length of ¾ in. Total of 3-6, with 1-2 broods.

FEEDER BEHAVIOR: Does not visit feeders.

COMPARE TO SIMILAR SPECIES: Orange underside and long, forked tail are very different than those of most other swallows. Cliff and Cave Swallows may have some orange on underside, but are much smaller and lack a strongly forked tail.

DID YOU KNOW? Unmated males sometimes enter the nests of established breeding pairs, killing all of the nestlings. This allows the encroacher to then breed with the previously mated female, often producing a second, viable brood.

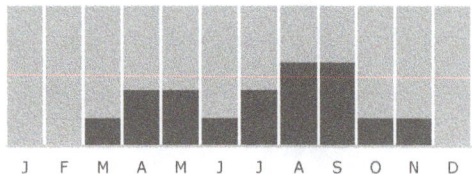

J F M A M J J A S O N D

Adults at top and bottom left,
Silhouette in flight at bottom right.

Breeding adult at top (Note: This individual's legs have been banded for research puposes),
Nonbreeding adult at bottom.

① SEMIPALMATED PLOVER.
Charadrius semipalmatus.

SIZE: 7 in.

HABITAT: Mostly beaches and mudflats. During migration, this may include locations along a variety of smaller lakes, reservoirs, and even flooded fields; however, wintering sites are more strictly limited to oceanic coastlines.

WILD DIET: Worms, aquatic invertebrates, and insects.

BEHAVIOR: This shorebird species is often observed in loose flocks, foraging along intertidal zones or mudflats for stranded worms and invertebrates. Individuals frenetically run, pause, and repeat as they scan for potential prey items—seldom wading into water more than an inch deep. The plovers peck in the direction of any movement in the substrate, with keen eyesight enabling the detection of worms and invertebrates up to a few inches below the surface. Call is a squeaky, rising *chweep*, which may also be uttered while foraging.

MIGRATE? Partially.

NESTING: Breeds along the tundral wetlands of northern Canada and Alaska. A very shallow nest scrape is made in the gravel, and lined with twigs and other vegetative debris. About 3 in. across.

EGGS: Off-white, with large dark spotting. Length of 1 ½ in. Total of 4.

FEEDER BEHAVIOR: Does not visit feeders.

COMPARE TO SIMILAR SPECIES: Similar to the much larger Killdeer, but has brighter orange legs, and only features one dark breast band (rather than two).

DID YOU KNOW? The Semipalmated Plover is named for the partial webbing present between its toes. This allows the plover to swim across narrow channels of water while foraging, though it seems to rarely employ this faculty—instead, normally taking short flights between feeding or roosting areas.

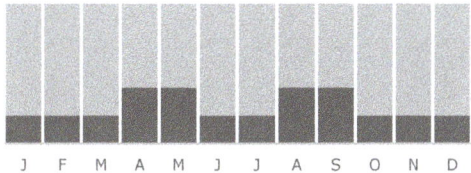

J F M A M J J A S O N D

① SUMMER TANAGER. *Piranga rubra.*

SIZE: 7 in.

HABITAT: Open woods, sometimes suburbs.

WILD DIET: Insects (e.g., wasps, bees) and spiders, sometimes fruit.

BEHAVIOR: A canopy-dwelling species, the Summer Tanager forages for insects by walking across branches, or by undertaking quick flights out into the open to snatch prey in midair. During breeding season, may be observed chasing away fellow tanagers or even cowbirds, the latter of which is rightly recognized as a threat to the nest. Song is vaguely similar to that of American Robin, but more slurred and less symmetrical in pitch.

MIGRATE? Partially.

NESTING: Selects a high fork in the branches of a tree, often situated over a clearing. Thick, shallow bowl woven with grasses and fine twigs. About 4 in. across.

EGGS: Deep sky blue, with dark brown speckling. Length of 1 in. Total of 3-4, occasionally with a second brood.

BIRD FEEDING TIPS

FEEDER DIET: Fruit, grape jelly, mealworms, suet. **FEEDER TYPES**: Platforms. **FEEDER BEHAVIOR**: Very uncommon visitor, and most likely to only visit for short intervals in late spring.

COMPARE TO SIMILAR SPECIES: Most similar to the related Scarlet Tanager; males lack jet-black wings and tail, while females tend to lack the greener back of the Scarlet. Bright red coloration of males might also suggest a Northern Cardinal, though this other species has a distinctive head crest and a frequently more upright posture.

DID YOU KNOW? Like its cousin, the Scarlet Tanager, this species scrapes wasps and bees against tree branches to remove the stinger before consumption.

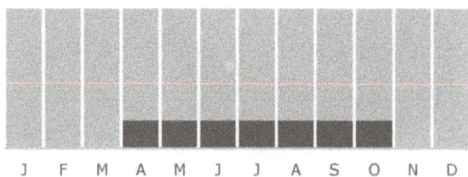

J F M A M J J A S O N D

Male at top,
Female at bottom.

Adult at top,
Juvenile at bottom.

② CEDAR WAXWING. *Bombycilla cedrorum.*

SIZE: 6 ½ in.

HABITAT: Open woods, orchards, overgrown fields, and suburbs.

WILD DIET: Primarily fruit and berries. Also, some insects during breeding season.

BEHAVIOR: This frugivorous species is most often found wherever wild fruits and berries are available. Forages for berries by hovering or stooping down from a branch; when pursuing insects, makes darting, agile flights from exposed perches. Congregates in medium to large-sized flocks, though some birds may wander a few hundred feet away near the fringes. Calls are repeated, high-pitched *tsee* notes.

MIGRATE? Yes.

NESTING: In a fork of tree branches, constructs a bowl of variable depth using woven twigs and grasses. About 5 in. across.

EGGS: Shades of blue-green, with dark spots. Length of ¾ in. Total of 4-7, occasionally with a second brood.

BIRD FEEDING TIPS

FEEDER DIET: Fruit. **FEEDER TYPES**: Platforms. **FEEDER BEHAVIOR**: Extremely uncommon at feeders, but likely to repeatedly visit yards with extensive plantings of native berry bushes and trees. However, do *not* plant the ornamental shrub *Nandina domestica*, also known as heavenly bamboo, as its berries are highly toxic to waxwings and other frugivorous (i.e., fruit-eating) birds.

COMPARE TO SIMILAR SPECIES: Closely resembles the Bohemian Waxwing, which is native to the evergreen forests of southern and central Canada, and may wander south in winters if there is an insufficient food supply. The Bohemian is much stouter, and has a grayish (rather than yellow) belly.

DID YOU KNOW? Waxwings are well-known for their habit of inadvertently consuming large quantities of overripe—and, therefore, fermenting—berries, a behavior which causes acute onset drunkenness. As a result, individuals may stagger about, fly repeatedly into cars and windows, and generally create a considerable hullabaloo.

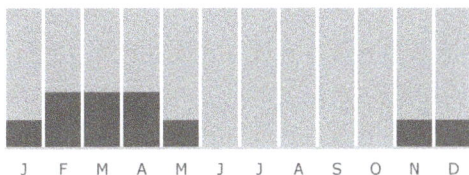

J F M A M J J A S O N D

231

③ **COMMON GROUND DOVE.**
Columbina passerina.

SIZE: 6 ½ in.

HABITAT: Desert scrubland, open woods, suburbs, and agricultural fields.

WILD DIET: Small seeds (i.e., those produced by various wild grasses) and grains, sometimes small berries and insects.

BEHAVIOR: This sparrow-sized dove tends to forage across the ground, but may be found hidden amid ground shrubs or perched in trees. Like most doves, its lethargy between foraging sessions tends to leave individuals especially prone to attack by all manner of raptors and mammals; in addition, the Common Ground Dove's small size means that even blackbirds and corvids (e.g., jays and crows) are occasionally apt to strike. Coo is a slow, repeated, and ascending *whooop*.

MIGRATE? Mostly not. May move locally between elevations or across topographical features.

NESTING: Usually located in fields at ground level, but may also be placed in bushes. Shallow bowl thatched with twigs and dried grasses. About 3 in. across.

EGGS: Bright white. Length of ¾ in. Total of 2, with 2-3 broods.

BIRD FEEDING TIPS

FEEDER DIET: Black-oil and hulled sunflower seeds, nyjer, millet, milo. **FEEDER TYPES**: Ground, platforms, hoppers. **FEEDER BEHAVIOR**: Often searches for fallen seeds or grains beneath feeders, though platforms and certain hoppers may also be appealing. Less likely to visit poorly placed feeder stations without adequate nearby shrub cover.

COMPARE TO SIMILAR SPECIES: Smaller than the Inca Dove, and lacks its relative's well-defined scalloped plumage on the back and wings.

DID YOU KNOW? In the Deep South, this bird has been given the sobriquet of "tobacco dove" on account of its particular affinity for nesting among crop fields.

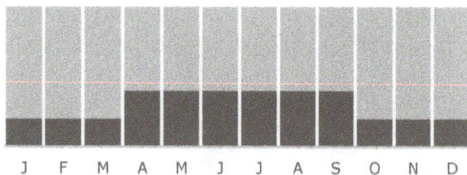

J F M A M J J A S O N D

Adults at top and bottom.

Adult male at top (Notice red on back of head),
Adult female at bottom.

④ DOWNY WOODPECKER. *Dryobates pubescens.*

SIZE: 6 ¼ in.

HABITAT: Open woods, suburbs.

WILD DIET: Mostly insects. Also, nuts (e.g., acorns), seeds, and berries.

BEHAVIOR: The smallest of the North American woodpeckers, this sparrow-sized bird is most often found industriously pecking away at tree bark. The beetles, ants, and larvae which are most often gleaned during this process constitute the majority of its diet, though this species is an exceedingly common backyard feeder visitor (particularly in winter). Commonly gives a high, squeaky *pic* call, and forms flocks much more readily than most other woodpecker species.

MIGRATE? Partially.

NESTING: Excavates a small cavity beneath a knob, often in a decaying tree. About 1 - 1 ½ in. across and 9 in. deep.

EGGS: White. Length of ¾ in. Total of 4-6, occasionally with a second brood.

BIRD FEEDING TIPS

FEEDER DIET: Suet, black-oil and hulled sunflower seeds, peanuts and peanut hearts, mealworms, safflower seed. **FEEDER TYPES:** Suet cages, hoppers, platforms, tubes. **FEEDER BEHAVIOR:** Acrobatically clings to hoppers or tubes, or pecks at suet cages. May arrive in small flocks if sufficient food sources available. During the breeding season, may be observed entertainingly chasing its conspecifics around and among the trees.

COMPARE TO SIMILAR SPECIES: Most similar to the larger Hairy Woodpecker, which is taller than the height of a standard suet cage. Downy has a bill shorter than the length of its head, and black spotting on its outer white tail feathers.

DID YOU KNOW? The Downy is a well-known predator of larvae of the invasive European corn borer, a moth which causes over $1 billion in yearly damages to the North American agricultural industry. This moth lays its eggs on the ears of corn, and larvae burrow into the crop as they rapidly mature and metamorphose.

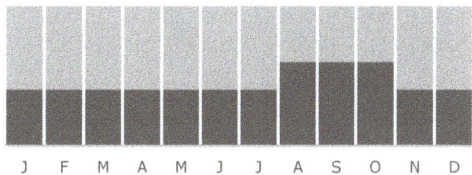

J F M A M J J A S O N D

④ **HOUSE SPARROW.** *Passer domesticus.*

SIZE: 6 ¼ in.

HABITAT: Cities, suburbs, farms.

WILD DIET: Seeds, grains, garbage, insects and spiders.

BEHAVIOR: If sparrows are present on a sidewalk or flowerbed in any variety of urban environment, they are almost always members of this invasive species. House Sparrows tend to form large, noisy flocks, which feature surprisingly rigid hierarchical structures: older males have more black on the breast and throat, while younger individuals may tremulously flick their tails when approached by elders. Between foraging sessions, several dozen individuals may perch in nearby trees or bushes. Vocalizations are a mix of *chrip* and *churrip* notes.

MIGRATE? No.

NESTING: Often colonial. Uses natural and manmade cavities, such as tree hollows, eaves of houses, and dilapidated roofs. A tight cup of grasses and stems is lined with feathers, and may be adjacent to another nest. About 5 in. wide.

EGGS: Off-white to light blue-green, with brown speckling. Length of ¾ in. Total of 4-6. Raises 2-4 broods each year, usually 3.

BIRD FEEDING TIPS

FEEDER DIET: Black-oil and hulled sunflower seeds, millet, peanut hearts, cracked corn, milo, suet. **FEEDER TYPES**: Ground, platforms, hoppers, tubes. **FEEDER BEHAVIOR**: Often present in large, semi-localized flocks, which may overrun feeders. May claim, and even evict existing tenants of, nest boxes.

COMPARE TO SIMILAR SPECIES: Compared to New World sparrows and finches, the black throat and breast of male are distinctive. Generally, its habitat and chunky profile are the clearest giveaways, along with the presence of nearby, identifiable males.

DID YOU KNOW? House Sparrows, even if fully or partially blinded, are able to maintain a consistent circadian rhythm, owing to photoreceptors located inside the skull.

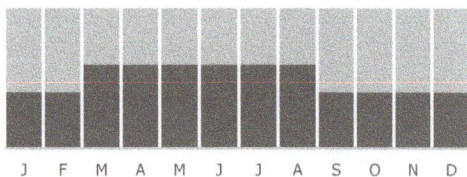

J F M A M J J A S O N D

Adult male at top,
Adult female at bottom.

Adult male at top (Photo by Andrew Weitzel / CC BY-SA / Cropped),
Adult female at bottom (Photo by Katja Schulz / CC BY-SA).

② **BLUE GROSBEAK.** *Passerina caerulea.*

SIZE: 6 ¼ in.

HABITAT: Thickets, open woods, and scrub. Sometimes, agricultural fields.

WILD DIET: Insects (e.g., crickets) and spiders, snails, seeds, grains, and fruit.

BEHAVIOR: Warbles and chinks amid dense tangles of vines and saplings, making this bird elusive in the field—and particularly difficult to clearly photograph. Usually forages by hopping on the ground, snatching small invertebrates and fallen plant matter from pockets in the brush. From late spring through summer, males sing from exposed perches while defending individual territories of up to 25 acres, leading to lower relative population densities. Most likely to flock during migration.

MIGRATE? Yes.

NESTING: Selects a secluded location less than 10 ft. above the ground, in branches of trees or shrubs. Neatly woven cup of twigs and stems. About 3-4 in. across.

EGGS: Off-white to light blue-green. Length of ¾ in. Total of 3-5, with 2 broods.

BIRD FEEDING TIPS

FEEDER DIET: Black-oil and hulled sunflower seeds, cracked corn, millet, oats, milo. **FEEDER TYPES**: Ground, platforms. **FEEDER BEHAVIOR**: Most likely to visit feeders in late summer or early fall—just before migration—as it tops off energy stores for the long flights ahead.

COMPARE TO SIMILAR SPECIES: Male and female resemble their Indigo Bunting counterparts, but note the following: Blue Grosbeaks are larger with a much more sizable bill, and the male is a deeper blue (i.e., indigo, rather than cerulean).

DID YOU KNOW? A flock of grosbeaks is known as a "gross." This also applies to other grosbeak species, such as the Pine and Rose-breasted varieties.

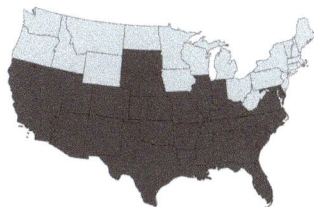

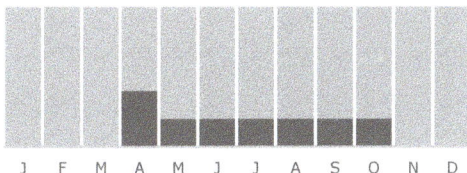

J F M A M J J A S O N D

④ EASTERN PHOEBE. *Sayornis phoebe.*

SIZE: 6 in.

HABITAT: Suburbs, open woods, field edges. Sometimes near sources of water.

WILD DIET: Flying insects. In colder months, may eat small fruits or berries.

BEHAVIOR: This dusky, solitary bird may initially seem inconspicuous for passive observers; however, it is among the first migrants to arrive in the spring, and perches on open branches while mirthfully bobbing its tail up and down. After frequent, darting flights out for prey, it almost always returns to the same perch, though it may select a new perch if insects are no longer present nearby. Its penchant for inhabiting open areas near houses, particularly during spring and fall migration, means that suburbanites will quickly grow familiar with this species' raspy, whistled *fee-bree*—repeated in tidy couplets all throughout the day.

MIGRATE? Yes.

NESTING: Prefers a rocky nook or cranny, often under manmade overhangs (e.g., eaves of roofs, fissures in concrete, etc.). Bowl of dried grasses and vegetation. About 6 in. across.

EGGS: Off-white to light pink, with mild speckling. Length of ¾ in. Total of 3-5, with 2 broods.

FEEDER BEHAVIOR: Does not normally visit feeders, though there have been rare reports of this species taking dried mealworms when food is scarce. May use nest boxes.

COMPARE TO SIMILAR SPECIES: The Eastern Wood-Pewee is of similar size and coloration. In particular, note the Eastern Phoebe's more slumped posture, darker head cap, and short, black bill.

DID YOU KNOW? Eastern Phoebes have successfully adapted their nesting habits to the ever-increasing presence of humankind, having previously used sheltered, rocky ledges. Some phoebes have even been observed nesting in the spaces vacated by fallen bricks in below-ground wells.

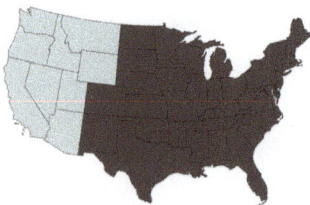

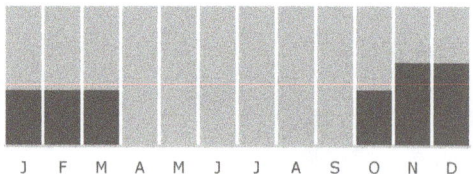

J F M A M J J A S O N D

Adult at top,
Juvenile at bottom (Notice light yellow on belly).

Adults at top and bottom.

④ TUFTED TITMOUSE. *Baeolophus bicolor.*

SIZE: 6 in.

HABITAT: Dense woods, wooded parks, and suburbs.

WILD DIET: Insects (e.g., caterpillars, wasps) and spiders, nuts (e.g., acorns), seeds, berries.

BEHAVIOR: A lively, nimble bird of the forests, this species restlessly flits from branch to branch: only taking fitful spells of rest when plotting its next foraging expeditions. Titmice are known to store seeds and nuts in the interstices of tree bark during fall and winter, often shelling them beforehand to allow for easy meals in the colder days ahead. Individuals also tend to select the largest seeds that will fit in their beaks, and peck them apart while pinning them to a perch with their feet. Song is a pellucid, high-whistled series of *pe-ter, pe-ter, pe-ter*, and calls include nasal buzzes and rasps similar to those of chickadees.

MIGRATE? No.

NESTING: Cavity nester. Uses tree hollows and former woodpecker nests, as well as small manmade cavities. A messy cup of grasses, mosses, and occasionally snake skins is constructed inside, and lined with animal hairs. About 4 in. wide.

EGGS: Off-white, with red or brown speckling. Length of ¾ in. Total of 3-8, sometimes with a second brood.

BIRD FEEDING TIPS

FEEDER DIET: Black-oil and hulled sunflower seeds, peanuts and peanut hearts, safflower seed, suet, mealworms. **FEEDER TYPES**: Platforms, hoppers, tubes, suet cages. **FEEDER BEHAVIOR**: Rarely stays for more than a few seconds during each visit, quickly finding a choice tidbit to store or consume nearby. Also, may use nest boxes.

COMPARE TO SIMILAR SPECIES: Black-crested Titmouse of Texas has a conspicuous, isolated dark crest. Much smaller and paler than Eastern Bluebird, with a fully white underside.

DID YOU KNOW? With the help of bird feeders, this species has expanded its original, more southerly range to include much of the Great Lakes and Northeast.

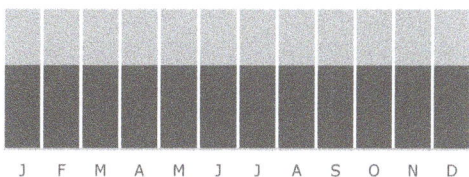

J F M A M J J A S O N D

② **SONG SPARROW.** *Melospiza melodia.*

SIZE: 5 ¾ in.

HABITAT: Thickets, hedgerows, overgrown fields, wetlands, open woods, parks. Very common in suburbs.

WILD DIET: Seeds (e.g., of grasses), fruits and berries, grains, insects and spiders.

BEHAVIOR: The most common sparrow across much of North America, this small, streaked species is ordinarily found skulking about brushy sections of habitat. In spring, the male spectacularly sings from exposed perches in bushes and small trees, with more exacting refrains preferred by potential female mates. Song is a sweet, multi-phrase melody of chips, whistles, buzzes, and trills.

MIGRATE? Yes.

NESTING: Usually placed on the ground in brushy or grassy areas, sometimes in a garden. Nest is cup-shaped, and woven with fine grasses. About 5-7 in. wide.

EGGS: Shades of blue-green, with brown speckling. Length of ¾ in. Total of 2-5, with 2-3 broods.

BIRD FEEDING TIPS

FEEDER DIET: Millet, milo, black-oil and hulled sunflower seeds, nyjer, peanut hearts, cracked corn, safflower seed, suet. **FEEDER TYPES**: Ground, platforms, hoppers, tubes. **FEEDER BEHAVIOR**: Very common on the ground beneath feeders, where it may take refuge in nearby cover between foraging sessions. Well-planted yards usually attract more individuals.

COMPARE TO SIMILAR SPECIES: Very similar to the Savannah Sparrow, which is instead found in open fields. May also resemble the Lincoln's Sparrow, which has a bolder topmost head stripe and a yellow tinge to the breast. Compared to female House and Purple Finches, this species has cleaner underside streaking and a less stout bill.

DID YOU KNOW? Song Sparrows successfully diminish the risks of predation and cowbird parasitism on their ground-based nests by laying several clutches of eggs throughout the late spring and summer.

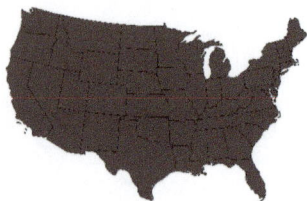

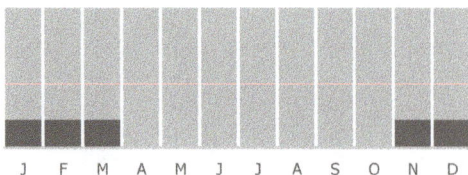

J F M A M J J A S O N D

Adults at top and bottom.

Adults at top and bottom.

② EASTERN WOOD-PEWEE. *Contopus virens.*

SIZE: 5 ½ in.

HABITAT: Variety of woods, but most frequently open, deciduous woods or edges of woods.

WILD DIET: Insects. Rarely, small fruits and berries.

BEHAVIOR: Selects elevated, well-visible perches from which to repeatedly sally out into the open for flying insects (e.g., dragonflies, wasps), occasionally stooping to vegetation or near the ground for wingless insects. Returns to the same perch after each flight; if an insect has been caught, it is repeatedly bludgeoned against the perch until it has been readied for consumption. Often hunts in the mid-canopy, beneath the domain of the Great Crested Flycatcher, but above that of the Least Flycatcher. Well-known for its ascending, high-whistled *pee-a-weee* call, which is sometimes audible for hundreds of feet.

MIGRATE? Yes.

NESTING: Nests at the confluence of several branches, about 30-60 ft. high. Finely woven cup of dried grasses and plant fibers. About 2 in. across.

EGGS: Off-white, with some rufous speckling. Length of ¾ in. Total of 2-4.

FEEDER BEHAVIOR: Does not visit feeders.

COMPARE TO SIMILAR SPECIES: To separate from *Empidonax* flycatchers, note that this species returns frequently to the same, conspicuous perch, and seldom flicks its tail. Possesses more defined white wing bars and an often sleeker silhouette than the Eastern Phoebe. Overall, characteristic song is highly diagnostic, especially when distinguishing from the Western Wood-Pewee in the Great Plains states.

DID YOU KNOW? Male wood-pewees aggressively defend a breeding territory of about 10 acres, and sometimes father two nests—each with a different female.

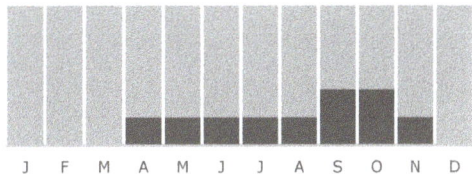

J F M A M J J A S O N D

④ **HOUSE FINCH.** *Carpodacus mexicanus*.

SIZE: 5 ½ in.

HABITAT: Cities and suburbs, open woods.

WILD DIET: Grains, seeds, and berries.

BEHAVIOR: Forages for food on the ground or in shrubbery, and perches in trees. Readily adapts to human habitation, often flocking in the vicinity of known feeders. Sings with complex, warbling melodies; calls with a sharp, ascending, and yanking tone.

MIGRATE? No.

NESTING: Openings in buildings, in shrubs or trees, or in outdoor décor. Cup-shaped; formed from small twigs and debris. About 6 in. across, and often 5-10 ft. above the ground.

EGGS: Off-white to light blue or green, with some dark speckling. Length of ¾ in. Total of 3-5, with 2-3 broods.

BIRD FEEDING TIPS

FEEDER DIET: Black-oil and hulled sunflower seeds, nyjer, safflower seed. **FEEDER TYPES**: Platforms, ground, hoppers, tubes. **FEEDER BEHAVIOR**: Can accumulate in flocks of several dozen, jostling for position but remaining present for several minutes or more. May outcompete other species when found in sufficient numbers.

COMPARE TO SIMILAR SPECIES: Purple Finch males have little to no streaking on the lower belly and have darker red coloration that runs from the head into wings and back; females have a pronounced pale eyebrow. By contrast, House Finches generally have a dirtier, more heavily streaked lower belly and a more shallowly forked tail; in addition, males have *no red on the folded wings* and females *lack well-defined striping across the side of head*. Sparrows generally have daintier bills.

DID YOU KNOW? House Finches are only native to the western half of the U.S. Following illegal sales in the pet trade during the 1940s, they colonized the entire eastern U.S., working their way westward from New York City before finally reuniting with their relatives near the Rocky Mountains around the year 2000.

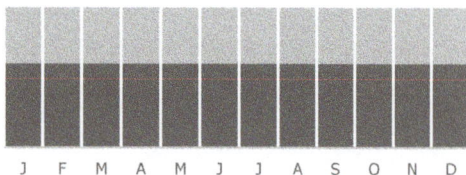

J F M A M J J A S O N D

Male at top,
Female at bottom.

Breeding adults at top,
Nonbreeding adults at bottom.

② LEAST SANDPIPER. *Calidris minutilla.*

SIZE: 5 ½ in.

HABITAT: Mudflats on edges of lakes, rivers, ponds, wetlands, and flooded fields.

WILD DIET: Insects and insect larvae, as well as very small aquatic invertebrates (e.g., snails).

BEHAVIOR: Probes the mud for small prey items buried in the substrate. Though it prefers mudflats, it also enters the inch-deep shallows of nearby water. Found in small to medium-sized groups, and may flock with other similarly sized shorebirds. Easily flushed if approached too closely, with individuals taking a somewhat direct path to another nearby foraging site. Along with the Spotted Sandpiper, this species is among the most common of all inland shorebirds.

MIGRATE? Yes.

NESTING: Breeds in the far north of Canada and Alaska. Forms a cuplike depression among stalks of thick grasses. About 2-3 in. across.

EGGS: Off-white with brown mottling. Length of 1 in. Total of 3-4.

FEEDER BEHAVIOR: Does not visit feeders.

COMPARE TO SIMILAR SPECIES: Other small "peep" sandpipers are often similar, but the Least is smallest and has *yellow legs*. Among breeding adults, the brown of its folded wings, back, and head cap is darker than that of the Semipalmated Sandpiper. Nonbreeding adults have a buffy band across the entire width of the breast and feature a darker gray-brown back, unlike the pale gray of the Western Sandpiper or the medium gray of the Semipalmated.

DID YOU KNOW? Though the smallest shorebird in the world, some individuals of this species have been known to undertake nonstop migratory flights exceeding 2,000 miles.

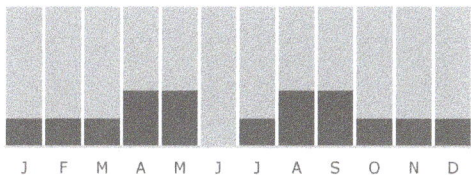

J F M A M J J A S O N D

251

① **SAVANNAH SPARROW.**
Passerculus sandwichensis.

SIZE: 5 ½ in.

HABITAT: Agricultural fields, grasslands, pastures.

WILD DIET: Seeds (e.g., of grasses), insects and spiders.

BEHAVIOR: Able to walk or hop along the ground while foraging, this sparrow chases down terrestrial insects or snatches seeds from overhanging grasses. Normally feeds solitarily or in very small groups, but may flock during migration or winter. In the spring, males tend to sing from elevated perches throughout their territories, offering an exceptional opportunity to observe this normally furtive species for lengthier periods of time. Its song consists of a short series of high chips and buzzes.

MIGRATE? Yes.

NESTING: On the ground amid dense grasses, occasionally sheltered by a nearby bush. Builds a finely woven cup of dried grasses and stems, which often has a thin, laterally extending lip. About 4 in. wide.

EGGS: Pale blue, blue-green, reddish-brown, pink, or off-white. Often features dark splotching. Length of ¾ in. Total of 2-5, with 1-2 broods.

FEEDER BEHAVIOR: Unlikely to visit feeders.

COMPARE TO SIMILAR SPECIES: May resemble other brown, streaked sparrows. Notice the Savannah's variably yellow lores (between the eye and bill), and its cleanly white-and-brown streaked chest.

DID YOU KNOW? There are as many as 17 recognized subspecies of Savannah Sparrow, perhaps owing to its tendency to breed in the very same localities where it hatched. Over time, this results in individual populations which grow genetically insular, thus accentuating their own divergent physical traits.

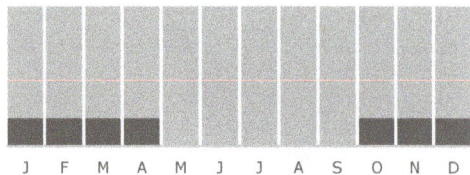

J F M A M J J A S O N D

Adults at top and bottom.

Breeding adult at top,
Nonbreeding adult at bottom.

③ CHIPPING SPARROW. *Spizella passerina.*

SIZE: 5 ½ in.

HABITAT: Open woods, parks, cities and suburbs.

WILD DIET: Seeds (e.g., of dandelions, wild buckwheat), insects and spiders.

BEHAVIOR: This spirited sparrow of the suburbs is ubiquitous in its favored habitat: hopping along near edges of lawns, perching in trees and shrubs, and gathering in small, loose flocks near feeders. Often prefers to perch between foraging sessions in sheltered, dense evergreens, if available. Song is a series of chipped, almost insect-like trills, which lasts up to five or six seconds.

MIGRATE? Yes.

NESTING: Selects a chest-high fork of branches in a shrub or tree, usually an evergreen. Height may be as low as one foot—or as high as 15 feet—above the ground. A cup is woven of twigs, grasses, and rootlets. About 5 in. across.

EGGS: Light blue or off-white, with brown spotting. Length of ¾ in. Total of 2-6, with 2 broods.

BIRD FEEDING TIPS

FEEDER DIET: Millet, milo, nyjer, hulled sunflower seeds. **FEEDER TYPES**: Hoppers, tubes, platforms, ground. **FEEDER BEHAVIOR**: Very common feeder visitor, and may also nest in a backyard tree or hedgerow. Gathers for moderate periods on smaller feeders, and may also loiter on the ground if fallen seed is present.

COMPARE TO SIMILAR SPECIES: During the breeding season, this species' rufous crest resembles that of the Field Sparrow, but note the black eyeline and long, white eyebrow of the Chipping (in addition to the fact that the Field is more common in open, rural grasslands).

DID YOU KNOW? Like many other birds, this species migrates by night—and, in fact, ranks as one of the most common such migrants. Ornithological sound technicians have been able to deduce species frequency patterns at a given site by counting nocturnal flight calls; usually, about 10 brief, high-pitched chips per hour can be easily heard for this species, and occasionally over 150 Chipping Sparrows per hour are logged.

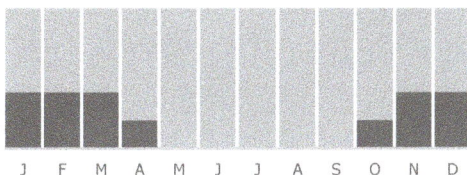

J F M A M J J A S O N D

② **RED-EYED VIREO.** *Vireo olivaceus.*

SIZE: 5 ½ in.

HABITAT: Mature, old-growth, usually deciduous woods. During migration, also in open woods, parks, and suburbs.

WILD DIET: Mostly insects (e.g., caterpillars, flies) and spiders, but also fruits and berries (particularly before and during migration).

BEHAVIOR: This prodigious melodist is capable of generating numerous ditties over the course of a day, usually from high in a mature, deciduous tree. Individuals tend to move more purposefully than many of the warblers and kinglets, with short investigatory hops along the branches of the canopy. Smaller insects are quickly snapped up, while caterpillars and grasshoppers may be pinned to the perch with one claw while consumed piecemeal. Occasionally, vireos may hover near the tips of branches to capture elusive insects on the undersides of foliage. Songs consist of short, up-and-down series of chirped or murmured notes, often repeated after a rest of no more than a few seconds.

MIGRATE? Yes.

NESTING: Selects a location in a deciduous tree, with branches or twigs forming part of the nest's rim. Nest hangs from these anchor points, and is partially suspended in midair. Woven with grasses and twigs, and thoroughly bound with spider webbing. About 3 in. across.

EGGS: White, with fine spotting. Length of ¾ in. Total of 2-4, with 1-2 broods.

FEEDER BEHAVIOR: Does not visit feeders.

COMPARE TO SIMILAR SPECIES: Very similar to other vireo species, such as the Warbling and Philadelphia. Note the dark-outlined, clearly defined pale eyebrow, which is most prominent in the Red-eyed, as well as the contrast between its grey head cap and light green back.

DID YOU KNOW? Red-eyed Vireos may sing as many as 50 distinct songs, and rarely cease vocalizing: with some birds singing over 20,000 times in a single day.

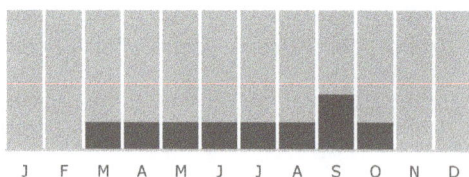

J F M A M J J A S O N D

Adults at top and bottom.

Adult male at top,
Adult female at bottom (Photo by Ken Gibson / CC BY-SA).

① **PINE WARBLER.** *Setophaga pinus.*

SIZE: 5 ½ in.

HABITAT: Open to semi-open pine woods. In migration, occasionally in mixed woods.

WILD DIET: Mostly insects (e.g., beetles, caterpillars, ants) and spiders. Particularly in winter, also seeds and fruits.

BEHAVIOR: This warbler is rather aptly named, considering its frequent associations with a variety of regional pine trees. Often forages by poking its bill into cones and in the nooks of branches, searching for various insects; these endeavors are normally undertaken relatively high in the canopy. Song is a chirping trill somewhat similar to that of the Chipping Sparrow, but slower and less mechanical.

MIGRATE? Partially.

NESTING: Selects a high, sheltered location in a pine tree. Nest is a wide cup of dried grasses, bound with caterpillar cocoons or spider silk. About 3 in. wide.

EGGS: Off-white, with brown blotching. Length of ¾ in. Total of 3-5, with 1-2 broods.

BIRD FEEDING TIPS

FEEDER DIET: Hulled sunflower seeds, mealworms, peanut hearts, suet. **FEEDER TYPES:** Hoppers, tubes, platforms, suet cages, ground. **FEEDER BEHAVIOR:** Most common early in migration or during winter, when individuals are somewhat less discerning with food selection. In winter, may loosely flock with chickadees or other warblers.

COMPARE TO SIMILAR SPECIES: Similar to a number of yellow-hued warbler species, including the Prairie, Yellow, Magnolia, and Blackpoll Warblers. To identify a Pine, notice the bold, yellow eye-ring (most pronounced on males), olive cheeks, and light streaking on the sides; also consider the specificity of its habitat.

DID YOU KNOW? This is the only warbler species which regularly consumes seeds—as one might surmise, these seeds are usually taken from pine cones.

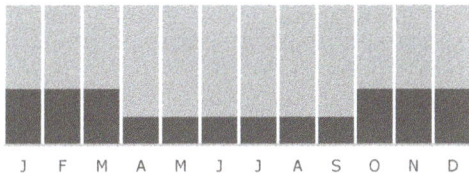

J F M A M J J A S O N D

① WHITE-BREASTED NUTHATCH.
Sitta carolinensis.

SIZE: 5 ¼ in.

HABITAT: Mature woods, either open or dense. Also, parks and suburbs.

WILD DIET: Insects (e.g., ants, larvae, caterpillars) and spiders, seeds and nuts.

BEHAVIOR: Nuthatches are often observed clinging upside-down to tree bark, periodically extending their heads outward to survey their surroundings. Short, firm hops allow individuals to descend the tree trunk or cling to branches, often in search of insects (in the summer) or seeds and nuts (winter). Throughout the colder months, often observed in larger mixed flocks with titmice and chickadees, which assist with locating food sources and maintaining a vigil for lurking predators: particularly Cooper's and Sharp-shinned Hawks. Also known for its raucous, nasally, and cackling *ha-a-a-a...* calls, which may echo for hundreds of feet.

MIGRATE? No, but short movements may sometimes occur in winter.

NESTING: Cavity nester. Uses natural tree hollows or former woodpecker nests, which can be rather more commodious than one might expect. A bowl of grasses and bark is lined with feathers. About 4-5 in. across.

EGGS: White, with russet spotting. Length of ¾ in. Total of 3-8.

BIRD FEEDING TIPS

FEEDER DIET: Black-oil and hulled sunflower seeds, peanuts and peanut hearts, suet, mealworms, safflower seed. **FEEDER TYPES**: Tubes, hoppers, suet cages, platforms. **FEEDER BEHAVIOR**: A series of brief visits allows this species to take large seeds and nuts, before pecking them apart (or "hatching" them) in the cranny of a tree; these may also be stored in bark crevices in late fall and winter. Also, sometimes uses nest boxes.

COMPARE TO SIMILAR SPECIES: Red-breasted Nuthatch is very similar, but has a dark black eyeline and orange underside. Chickadees may also resemble this species, but note the distinct differences in movement (i.e., rarely upside down).

DID YOU KNOW? Nuthatches roost alone in tree cavities; however, in very cold weather, up to a couple dozen may crowd together in a single roost for warmth.

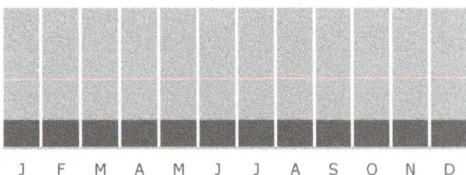

J F M A M J J A S O N D

Adult male at top (Note the black—rather than gray—cap),
Adult female at bottom.

Adults at top and bottom.

③ **CHIMNEY SWIFT.** *Chaetura pelagica.*

SIZE: 5 ¼ in.

HABITAT: Cities and suburbs, parks, and fields.

WILD DIET: Flying insects (e.g., flies, ants, beetles, wasps).

BEHAVIOR: Usually described as a "cigar with wings," this diminutive bird spends the entire day in the air. Low wing-loading allows for seemingly effortless flight: with alternating gliding and flitting of wings, and calls which resound with a barrage of chittering. May reach diving speeds of well over 100 mph, and typically observed at speeds of 30 to 75 mph in level flight. During breeding season, most swifts stay relatively close to colonial nest sites, though individuals may venture up to five miles away. Swifts are unable to perch, and exclusively cling vertically to hard surfaces at their roosting or nesting sites, which include the interiors of chimneys and hollowed-out tree trunks.

MIGRATE? Yes.

NESTING: Previously nested in caves and hollowed tree trunks; now, almost exclusively nests in uncovered chimney flues. Bowl of twigs is bound together and to the vertical surface with cement-like saliva. About 4 in. across.

EGGS: Bright white. Length of ¾ in. Total of 3-5.

FEEDER BEHAVIOR: Does not visit feeders.

COMPARE TO SIMILAR SPECIES: Short, stubby body and very long, narrow wings differentiate from various swallows and nightjars. Unlike bats, this species normally flies by light of day.

DID YOU KNOW? Particularly during migration, flocks of thousands of swifts often descend to a communal roost, such as a chimney or smokestack, en masse. This results in an enormous, funnel-like conglomeration which ranks among the most enrapturing spectacles in all of urban birdwatching.

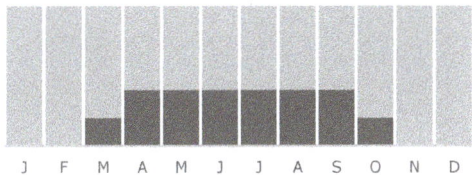

J F M A M J J A S O N D

④ YELLOW-RUMPED WARBLER.
Setophaga coronata.

SIZE: 5 ¼ in.

HABITAT: Open to semi-open woods. In winter, also suburbs, parks, and dunes.

WILD DIET: Mostly insects (e.g., beetles, caterpillars, aphids) and spiders. In winter, also fruits and berries (e.g., bayberry, juniper, poison ivy).

BEHAVIOR: An adaptable and varied forager, this species is known to plunder spider webs, catch flying insects which pass too close to an exposed perch, and cling to and probe the bark of trees—in addition to more customary warbler foraging habitats, such as hopping along and exploring branches. In winter, this species may consume copious amounts of berries, allowing it to stay much farther north than many other warblers. Song is a simple, burbling series.

MIGRATE? Yes.

NESTING: Selects a location atop a cluster of conifer branches. Twigs, grasses, and needles are used to loosely weave a cup-shaped nest. About 3-4 in. across.

EGGS: Off-white, with brown speckling. Length of ¾ in. Total of 3-5, occasionally with a second brood.

BIRD FEEDING TIPS

FEEDER DIET: Suet, mealworms, fruit, grape jelly, sugar water, black-oil and hulled sunflower seeds, peanut hearts. **FEEDER TYPES**: Hoppers, tubes, platforms, suet cages, nectar feeders, ground. **FEEDER BEHAVIOR**: An uncommon feeder visitor, this species is most likely to visit during migration or in winter. May be otherwise common in the backyard.

COMPARE TO SIMILAR SPECIES: Most similar to Magnolia and Yellow-throated Warblers. The Yellow-rumped has a conspicuous black mask, yellow rump, white belly (unlike the yellow belly of the Magnolia) and band of streaking across the breast (unlike the fully yellow throat and breast of the Yellow-throated).

DID YOU KNOW? The Yellow-rumped Warbler is split into two North American subspecies, the Myrtle and the Audubon's. Myrtle Warblers are pictured at left, and are more common east of the Rockies; while the Audubon's features a yellow (rather than white) throat, and is more common near the Rockies and in the West.

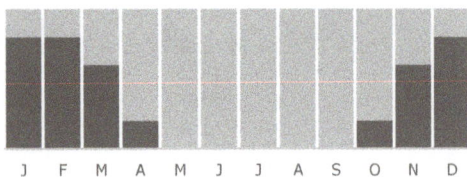

J F M A M J J A S O N D

Adult male at top,
Adult female at bottom left (Photo by Andrew Weitzel / CC BY-SA / Cropped),
Juvenile at bottom right.

Adults at top and bottom.

④ **CAROLINA WREN.** *Thryothorus ludovicianus.*

SIZE: 5 ¼ in.

HABITAT: Thickets and thicketed woods, overgrown fields, and brushy suburbs and parks.

WILD DIET: Mostly insects (e.g., beetles, grasshoppers) and spiders. Occasionally, small reptiles and amphibians, or seeds and berries.

BEHAVIOR: This large, loquacious wren is a well-known fixture of many eastern North American landscapes. More often heard than seen, it forages near to the ground amid dense cover—though it may occasionally be observed singing from an exposed perch. Its calls and songs are heard many hundreds, or even thousands, of times each day; these sweet, chattering, and whistled tunes may sound like *tea-kettle, tea-kettle, tea-kettle* or *chippery, chippery, chippery.*

MIGRATE? No.

NESTING: Cavity nester. Adaptive in its selection of cavity, with known locations including tree hollows, as well as flowerpots, mailboxes, or other artificial items. Nest cup features a partial arched roof, and is constructed with dried grasses and leaves. About 5 in. across, on average.

EGGS: White, with rusty speckling. Length of ¾ in. Total of 3-6, with 2-3 broods.

BIRD FEEDING TIPS

FEEDER DIET: Suet, mealworms, peanut hearts, black-oil and hulled sunflower seeds.
FEEDER TYPES: Platforms, suet cages, hoppers, tubes, ground. **FEEDER BEHAVIOR:** Uncommon visitor. May be observed taking suet from cages, or mealworms from small platform cups. Uses nest boxes and specially designed wren houses.

COMPARE TO SIMILAR SPECIES: Bold, white eyebrow and tawny chest best distinguish from most other wrens.

DID YOU KNOW? The Carolina Wren is the official state bird of South Carolina, and was even featured on the Palmetto State's special-edition quarter. This coin was minted in 2000 as the eighth of 50 state quarters to enter general circulation.

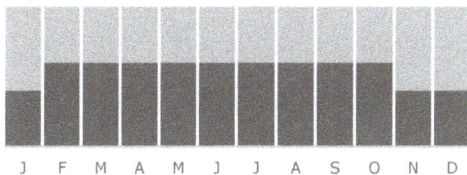

J F M A M J J A S O N D

② **INDIGO BUNTING.** *Passerina cyanea.*

SIZE: 5 ¼ in.

HABITAT: Mostly thickets and overgrown fields. Sometimes, edges of woods and roadsides; during migration, also suburbs, meadows, and open woods.

WILD DIET: Insects, seeds, berries, and grains.

BEHAVIOR: Forages low or along the ground in thickets, variably clinging to unstable stems and grasses as it cranes its neck to reach potential food sources. Normally found solitarily or in very small groups, aside from during migration. When singing (sometimes from elevated perches), note its high-pitched, coupled *whip, whip* or *chew, chew*, which forms the basis of longer melodic stanzas.

MIGRATE? Partially.

NESTING: Low to the ground, in a fork of dense vegetation. Cup-shaped, woven with grasses, and wrapped with spider webbing. About 2-3 in. across.

EGGS: White, sometimes with light brown spotting. Length of ¾ in. Total of 3-4, with 2 broods.

BIRD FEEDING TIPS

FEEDER DIET: Nyjer, millet, mealworms, milo, black-oil and hulled sunflower seeds, oats. **FEEDER TYPES:** Ground, tubes, hoppers, platforms. **FEEDER BEHAVIOR:** Most likely to visit in migration: sporadically in flocks of up to several dozen. Otherwise, uncommon.

COMPARE TO SIMILAR SPECIES: Key year-round differences from Lazuli Bunting of western North America include an absence of orange on the male's breast, and the lack of distinct wing bars on female. The Blue Grosbeak is also similar in appearance, but is larger and has a much stouter bill.

DID YOU KNOW? Indigo Buntings are the Galileans of the avian kingdom. During migration, which is undertaken by night, individuals accurately navigate by referencing the positions of the stars, even adjusting as constellations move over the course of weeks, seasons, and years. Indeed, captive buntings are even known to experience confusion if deprived of the ability to see the celestial lights.

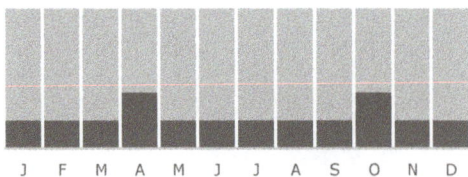

J F M A M J J A S O N D

Breeding male at top,
Nonbreeding male at bottom left,
Female at bottom right.

Adults at top and bottom.

③ **TREE SWALLOW.** *Tachycineta bicolor.*

SIZE: 5 in.

HABITAT: Fields, wetlands, and lakes.

WILD DIET: Mostly flying insects (e.g., dragonflies, ladybugs), sometimes egg shells and fish bones before egg-laying for added calcium. During cold snaps in its wintering range, may resort to consuming bayberries as well.

BEHAVIOR: Often observed perching on wires, branches, or fence posts, this species is common across its preferred habitat in most of North America. The Tree Swallow forages by gliding somewhat low over the ground, with occasional series of quick wingbeats to regain altitude and reorient its heading. Tends to flock more prolifically outside of breeding season, but loose groups may still be observed in the late spring to midsummer near optimal feeding sites. Calls are high-pitched, burbling, and echoing.

MIGRATE? Yes.

NESTING: Cavity nester. Uses a natural tree hollow, former woodpecker nest, or manmade nest box (sometimes a martin house); this site is usually close to water. Inside, a loose bowl is formed of dried grasses and aquatic reeds. About 4 in. wide.

EGGS: Bright white. Length of ¾ in. Total of 3-7.

FEEDER BEHAVIOR: Does not visit feeders, but does use nest boxes.

COMPARE TO SIMILAR SPECIES: Iridescent, blue-green back is highly distinctive among the North American swallows. Furthermore, this species is much smaller than the Purple Martin, and has a white, rather than dark, underside.

DID YOU KNOW? A single Tree Swallow may catch over one million flying insects in a single year, especially if feeding its hatchling young for a portion of the summer. When extrapolated to account for localized populations of several thousand individuals, one can easily see the extent to which this species is dependent on insect populations—which have fallen in the Tree Swallow's typical habitats by as much as one-half in the past 50 years.

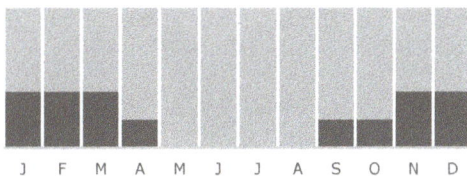

J F M A M J J A S O N D

④ **PALM WARBLER.** *Setophaga palmarum.*

SIZE: 5 in.

HABITAT: Open woods, overgrown fields, wetland edges. During migration, also parks and suburbs.

WILD DIET: Insects (e.g., beetles, flies) and spiders. In winter, sometimes berries.

BEHAVIOR: This warbler commonly hunts for insects along the ground or low in shrubs, merrily bobbing its tail as it walks or hops along. Individuals may select an exposed perch and chase after nearby flying insects. Not ordinarily found in groups during the warmer months, but may form larger mixed flocks with sparrows and other warblers on its wintering grounds. Song is a mechanical, monotonous, and rattling trill similar to that of the Chipping Sparrow.

MIGRATE? Yes.

NESTING: Breeds in northern coniferous forests; it selects a nesting location on the ground, at the base of a fern or shrub. A roughly hewn bowl of twigs and plant fibers is assembled. About 4-5 in. wide.

EGGS: White, with light brown blotches. Length of ¾ in. Total of 4-5, with 2 broods.

FEEDER BEHAVIOR: Rarely visits feeders.

COMPARE TO SIMILAR SPECIES: Most similar to the less common Prairie Warbler, which lacks the rufous head crown of the breeding Palm Warbler, as well as the pale eyebrow of the nonbreeding Palm.

DID YOU KNOW? The Palm Warbler's common name can be misleading, as individuals seldom associate with palm trees in their natural habitat. This name was given in 1789 by the German naturalist J.P. Gmelin, who located a wintering specimen on the Caribbean island of Hispaniola and subsequently named this warbler for the palms common to the surrounding area.

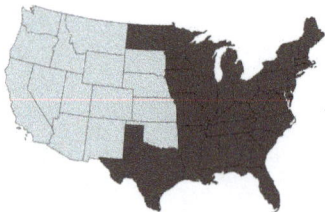

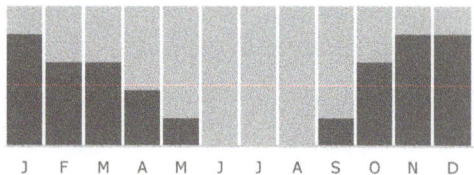

J F M A M J J A S O N D

Breeding adult at top,
Nonbreeding adult at bottom.

Male at top,
Female at bottom.

③ **PAINTED BUNTING.** *Passerina ciris.*

SIZE: 5 in.

HABITAT: Open woods with thickets, also overgrown fields.

WILD DIET: Seeds and insects.

BEHAVIOR: Mostly forages by itself, gleaning small seeds from twigs and grasses. Prefers to remain concealed in the forest understory or deep in thickets. Sometimes, takes to raiding spider webs for a free lunch. Males often defend territories of several acres, wounding any conspecific competitors who dare venture too close. Sings with thin, high whistles, or periodic, high *pwik* calls.

MIGRATE? Partially.

NESTING: Nests in the fork of a shrub or low tree. Nest is cup-shaped, and woven of fine grasses and fibers. Wrapped in spider webs. About 2-3 in. across.

EGGS: Off-white, with reddish-brown speckling—often more prominent along oblong edge. Length of ¾ in. Total of 3-4. Usually raises 2 broods each year, sometimes 3.

BIRD FEEDING TIPS

FEEDER DIET: Millet. **FEEDER TYPES**: Tubes, hoppers, ground. **FEEDER BEHAVIOR**: Most common during migration or winter. Can frequently be very picky in backyards, and prefers a feed mix which includes white proso millet. Requires nearby shelter.

COMPARE TO SIMILAR SPECIES: Both male and female are quite unique.

DID YOU KNOW? Speakers of other languages appear to be equally enthralled by this species' color palette. In Spanish, this bird is known as *el Azulillo Sietecolores,* or the "seven-colored bluebird;" in French, *le Passerin nonpareil* is the "passerine (or perching bird) without equal." Even the Greek *ciris* refers to the mythological tale of Princess Scylla of Megara, who absconded with a purple lock of hair before being punitively transformed into her eventual namesake bird.

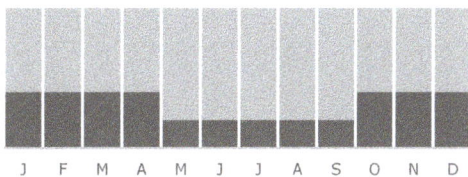

J F M A M J J A S O N D

③ WHITE-EYED VIREO. *Vireo griseus.*

SIZE: 5 in.

HABITAT: Thickets, overgrown fields, edges of woods.

WILD DIET: Mostly insects (e.g., caterpillars) and spiders, but also fruits and berries (particularly in fall and winter).

BEHAVIOR: The fierce countenance of the White-eyed Vireo belies its tendency to associate with dense, enshrouding thickets. As such, it is often difficult to catch a glimpse of this bird in the open, and may be easiest to recognize by song. Individuals deliberately scramble and flitter about through the brush, seeking out hidden insects—particularly caterpillars. Song is a bouncy, chirped *spit-a-phooey-phooey-spit!*, with the *spit* notes sometimes harsh and raspy.

MIGRATE? Partially.

NESTING: Selects a location between two intersecting branches, which form part of the nest's rim. Nest is hung from these anchoring points, and is cup-shaped. Constructed with fine grasses and plant fibers, and bound with several layers of spider silk, which may give the nest a frosted appearance. About 2-3 in. wide.

EGGS: White, with fine, well-spaced, and dark spotting. Length of ¾ in. Total of 2-5, with 1-2 broods.

FEEDER BEHAVIOR: Does not visit feeders.

COMPARE TO SIMILAR SPECIES: Bright yellow spectacles, along with a pale throat and chest, differentiate from other vireos. To distinguish from warblers, particularly note the much stouter bill characteristic to the vireo family.

DID YOU KNOW? Like the Red-eyed Vireo, this species' eye color changes over the course of its first year. Juvenile White-eyeds originally have dark brown eyes, which gradually transition to feature a pale or white iris by the following spring.

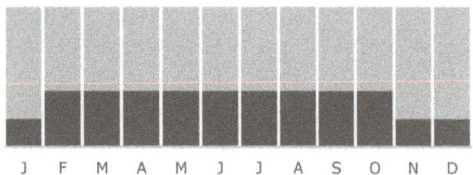

J F M A M J J A S O N D

Adults at top and bottom.

Breeding female at top,
Breeding male at bottom left,
Nonbreeding adult at bottom right.

③ AMERICAN GOLDFINCH. *Spinus tristis*.

SIZE: 5 in.

HABITAT: Overgrown fields and meadows, suburbs, and parks.

WILD DIET: Seeds (e.g., thistle, sunflower, dandelion, milkweed, alder).

BEHAVIOR: An active, social, and often highly visible finch, this species tends to hopscotch from plant to plant as it meticulously gleans the seeds which constitute the near entirety of its diet—a dietary trait known as *granivory*. Can be quite nimble in hanging from flowers and other seed heads, allowing this bird to reach a number of food sources that would be otherwise inaccessible. Sings with a high tone and cadence of *po-ta-to-chip*, and calls most frequently with a high, yanking duplet of whistles.

MIGRATE? Partially. Some individuals move southward if temperatures dip below freezing, and particularly if below zero.

NESTING: Usually in shrubbery or hedgerows, well elevated off the ground. Small cup woven of plant fibers, and lined with downy pollen. Anchored to branches with spider webbing. About 3 in. across.

EGGS: Off-white to light blue, with light spotting. Length of ¾ in. Total of 2-6, occasionally with a second brood.

BIRD FEEDING TIPS

FEEDER DIET: Nyjer, black-oil and hulled sunflower seeds. **FEEDER TYPES**: Tubes, hoppers, platforms, ground. **FEEDER BEHAVIOR**: Very common at feeders, and tends to loiter in the same manner as House Finches. Molt can be gradually observed in early spring, transitioning from drab buff into bright yellow as it triumphantly enters its breeding season.

COMPARE TO SIMILAR SPECIES: Most similar to the smaller Lesser Goldfinch of the West and Southwest. Notable differences include the American's bright yellow (in breeding season) or pale back (nonbreeding), and orange bill (breeding). In addition, the Lesser rarely, if ever, occurs northeast of Missouri.

DID YOU KNOW? The American Goldfinch is the state bird of Iowa, New Jersey, and Washington.

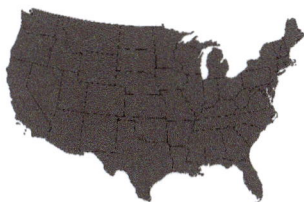

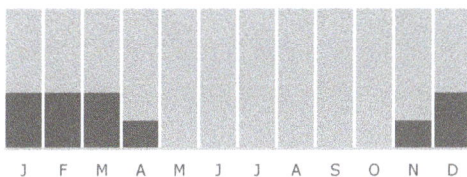

J F M A M J J A S O N D

② **AMERICAN REDSTART.** *Setophaga ruticilla.*

SIZE: 5 in.

HABITAT: Large tracts of semi-open woods, often with thickets and situated near water.

WILD DIET: Mostly insects (e.g., moths, flies, caterpillars) and spiders. In early fall, occasionally consumes berries and seeds.

BEHAVIOR: This boldly colored warbler with the show-stopping, fan-shaped tail gracefully flits like a butterfly throughout the forest understory. Somewhat uniquely for warblers, it catches most of its insects aerially with flycatcher-like sallies, though it also gleans directly from branches. When approaching a brushy area, individuals will often open or fan their tails, flushing any nearby insects with a bright flash of color. Song is a series of burry *zeets* and effervescent whistles.

MIGRATE? Yes.

NESTING: Situated in a vertical fork of tree branches, usually adjacent to the trunk. A cup is manufactured to conform to the fork, and is well-woven with fine plant fibers, often bound with lichens or the nest combs of paper wasps. About 3 in. across.

EGGS: Off-white, with heavy reddish-brown speckling. Length of ¾ in. Total of 2-5.

FEEDER BEHAVIOR: Does not visit feeders.

COMPARE TO SIMILAR SPECIES: The male Blackburnian Warbler has orange that is limited to the head and throat, contrasting with the male American Redstart's fully black head. This species' coloration is also similar to that of the Baltimore Oriole, but note the redstart's much smaller size and differing foraging habits.

DID YOU KNOW? In Jamaica, this species is commonly nicknamed the "latrine bird" for its partiality for hanging around outdoor toilets and garbage dumps. These sites predictably host a king's ransom of flies, which the wintering redstarts gleefully devour.

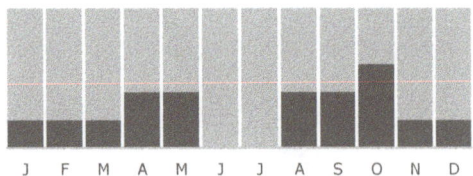

J F M A M J J A S O N D

Adult male at top,
Adult female at bottom.

Adults at top and bottom.

③ **HOUSE WREN.** *Troglodytes aedon*.

SIZE: 4 ¾ in.

HABITAT: Open woods, thickets, suburbs, parks, and gardens.

WILD DIET: Insects (e.g., caterpillars, ladybugs) and spiders (e.g., daddy longlegs).

BEHAVIOR: This species busily forages in the brushy understory of open woodland, searching for small, terrestrial insects and spiders. It is highly adaptable to various habitats, so long as they feature some brush or nearby thicket. Song is a burbling and rattling series of notes, which is typically only repeated throughout the spring and summer; in the spring, males frequently sing from elevated perches to attract mates, while females also sing during the nesting season to assert their dominance over the immediate area.

MIGRATE? Yes.

NESTING: Cavity nester. Selects a natural cavity, former woodpecker nest, or artificial substitute. A thin cup of twigs and grasses is lined with feathers. About 3-4 in. across.

EGGS: Off-white to light pink, with light speckling. Length of ¾ in. Total of 4-8, with 2 broods.

BIRD FEEDING TIPS

FEEDER DIET: Mealworms, suet. **FEEDER TYPES:** Platforms. **FEEDER BEHAVIOR:** Rare visitor. Most attracted by small platform cups filled with mealworms or bits of suet. Also, may use nest boxes and specially designed wren houses.

COMPARE TO SIMILAR SPECIES: Most similar to the regionally uncommon Winter Wren, which has dark belly streaking and is somewhat darker overall.

DID YOU KNOW? House Wrens are quite aggressive with regard to their nests. They have been known to fill the nests of nearby wrens with sticks, and even puncture their eggs. In addition, if a suitable nest cavity has already been taken, the female may displace the incumbent pair to take the location for herself.

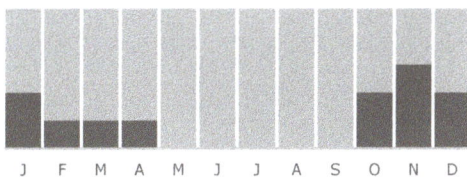

J F M A M J J A S O N D

283

② COMMON YELLOWTHROAT. *Geothlypis trichas.*

SIZE: 4 ¾ in.

HABITAT: Thickets, often near wetlands or edges of woods. May be observed in less densely thicketed areas during migration.

WILD DIET: Insects (e.g., beetles, ants, flies) and spiders.

BEHAVIOR: This species is often found scrambling about the low branches of damp thickets as it undertakes its daily foraging activities. The male's roguish mask is one of the most recognizable features on a North American warbler, and functions as a signal of masculine territoriality to its conspecifics. Song is a high, warbled series of *twiddly-twiddly-twiddly...*, which is very noticeable as males establish and maintain their breeding territories in late spring and summer.

MIGRATE? No.

NESTING: Near the ground, amid marshy vegetation. Nest is cup-shaped, and woven of dried reeds and stems. About 4 in. across.

EGGS: Off-white to light blue-green, with brown markings. Length of ¾ in. Total of 3-5, with 2 broods.

FEEDER BEHAVIOR: Rarely visits feeders, usually for suet.

COMPARE TO SIMILAR SPECIES: Male's black mask is fairly distinctive. Females are best distinguished by the combination of their yellow throat and breast, white belly, and olive back.

DID YOU KNOW? Of the billions of birds which migrate across the Gulf of Mexico each year, many fail to complete the parlous journey. As a result, tiger sharks—widely recognized for their wide-ranging eating habits, including the consumption of cans and license plates—have learned to congregate in certain sections of ocean where birds are most likely to fall, and Common Yellowthroats have been positively identified in the stomach contents of several analyzed tiger sharks.

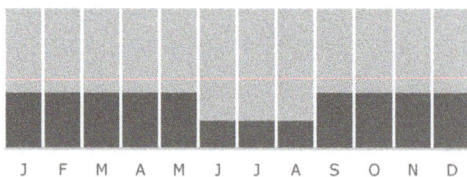

J F M A M J J A S O N D

Adult male at top,
Adult female at bottom.

Adult male at top (Note the black throat),
Adult female at bottom.

② BLACK-AND-WHITE WARBLER. *Mniotilta varia.*

SIZE: 4 ¾ in.

HABITAT: Wide variety of woods, including well-wooded suburbs.

WILD DIET: Insects (e.g., caterpillars, ants, beetles) and spiders.

BEHAVIOR: This species is rather unique among the warblers, in that it frequently forages by clinging to tree bark. This nuthatch-esque behavior can be quite entertaining to watch, with individuals often hanging from branches, scraping at bark, and generally making acrobats of themselves. To suit these eclectic habits, this species' toes—particularly the hind toe—are longer than other warblers', which allows for a secure grip on vertical surfaces. Throughout the spring and early summer, Black-and-whites primarily consume caterpillars, which may be located on the undersides of difficult-to-reach branches. Song is a high, quick, and repeated *wheezy, wheezy, wheezy.*

MIGRATE? Yes.

NESTING: Selects a concealed location on the ground. A wide-rimmed nest cup is constructed with leaves and grasses. About 4-5 in. wide.

EGGS: Off-white, with reddish speckling. Length of ¾ in. Total of 4-5, occasionally with a second brood.

FEEDER BEHAVIOR: Does not visit feeders.

COMPARE TO SIMILAR SPECIES: Most similar to the Blackpoll Warbler, which is also black and white. However, while the Black-and-white features a boldly striped head, the Blackpoll instead has a plain, black cap and a broad, white cheek.

DID YOU KNOW? While a flock of warblers is commonly known as a bouquet, wrench, or confusion, the Black-and-white has its own collective noun; ergo, a flock is known as a *dichotomy* of Black-and-white Warblers—referencing the rather binary coloration of its plumage.

④ CAROLINA CHICKADEE. *Poecile carolinensis*.

SIZE: 4 ½ in.

HABITAT: Various woods, parks, and suburbs. Range closely overlaps with that of the Black-capped Chickadee at the northern edge, as pictured and described at left.

WILD DIET: Insects (caterpillars, larvae) and spiders, seeds, nuts, and berries.

BEHAVIOR: Large, loose flocks of this species often maraud open wooded areas, nimbly perching and hanging from branches. Gleaned nuts and seeds are pinned to a branch with the feet, and broken open with the bill. The familiar *chick-a-dee-dee...* call of this species is higher and quicker than that of the Black-capped; in addition, the number of *dees* increases with the level of perceived danger.

MIGRATE? No.

NESTING: Cavity nester (e.g., self-excavated, or existing hollow or nest cavity). Inside, a cup is fashioned with plant fibers and lined with animal fur. About 4 in. wide.

EGGS: White, with reddish-brown spotting. Length of ½ in. Total of 3-8.

BIRD FEEDING TIPS

FEEDER DIET: Black-oil and hulled sunflower seeds, peanuts and peanut hearts, suet, mealworms, safflower seed, nyjer. **FEEDER TYPES**: Platforms, hoppers, tubes, suet cages. **FEEDER BEHAVIOR**: Briefly visits, before carrying away its haul to a nearby perch. Inquisitive, and may even approach humans. Occasionally uses nest boxes.

COMPARE TO SIMILAR SPECIES: Most similar to the slightly larger Black-capped Chickadee. Carolina has much finer, white (almost greyish) lines on its wing feathers, which are observable across its side when the wings are folded. Contrastingly, the Black-capped has thicker, bolder white markings on its folded wings.

DID YOU KNOW? Where the ranges of the Black-capped and Carolina Chickadees overlap, such as in the Greater Pittsburgh area, the two species readily interbreed and hybridize. This overlap zone is moving northward at a rate of approximately 10 to 15 miles per decade—primarily due to the effects of rising global temperatures.

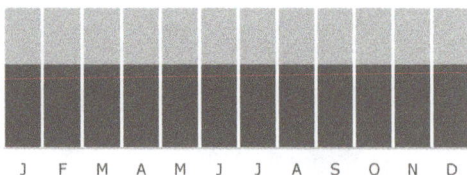

J F M A M J J A S O N D

Adults at top and bottom,
Species range map inset (Note: Green highlighting represents range of Carolina Chickadee, and
Black-capped/Carolina overlap zone occurs within a 25-mile-wide band north of the green area).

Adult male at top (Note the thick, black throat band),
Adult female at bottom.

② NORTHERN PARULA. *Setophaga americana.*

SIZE: 4 ½ in.

HABITAT: Mature, dense woods, often near water.

WILD DIET: Mostly insects (e.g., caterpillars, cicadas) and spiders. Occasionally, berries.

BEHAVIOR: The canopy-dwelling Northern Parula actively hops along branches as it forages, often targeting caterpillars and spiders. Wingbeats are quick as individuals fly between perches, making this bird seemingly appear as a blue flash as it bursts through gaps in the foliage. Like many warblers, this species tends to forage by itself or in pairs throughout much of the summer, and joins large, loose flocks during migration. Song is a buzzing trill, with a gradually rising glissando.

MIGRATE? Yes.

NESTING: Selects a high location amid hanging mosses or lichens (e.g., particularly Spanish moss, also Old Man's Beard lichen). Nest is an enclosed cup that is formed and hollowed out of a particularly thick clump of this hanging vegetation. About 4 in. wide.

EGGS: White, with red-brown spotting. Length of ¾ in. Total of 3-6, with 1-2 broods.

FEEDER BEHAVIOR: Does not visit feeders.

COMPARE TO SIMILAR SPECIES: This bird is impressively distinctive; notice the blue head and back, as well as the yellow throat and white belly.

DID YOU KNOW? The Northern Parula's penchant for treetop foraging has exacerbated many a case of *warbler neck*, a common orthopedic condition which temporarily causes stiffness of neck among birders. During migratory periods, when species diversity is often highest, many birders will crane their necks upwards for extended periods as they seek to build an impressive species count—an exercise which may be best accompanied by the application of an ice pack later in the day.

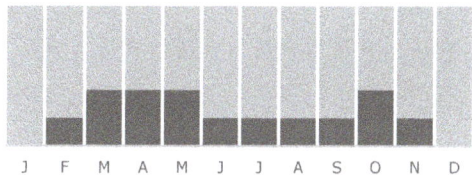

J F M A M J J A S O N D

③ BLUE-GRAY GNATCATCHER.
Polioptila caerulea.

SIZE: 4 ½ in.

HABITAT: Open woods, often with thickets and sometimes near water.

WILD DIET: Insects (e.g., grasshoppers, insect larvae) and spiders.

BEHAVIOR: This petite insectivore is often observed spreading, flicking, or cocking its tail as it moves along through the foliage, a mechanism which may help to flush any nearby insects. Otherwise, its insect prey is gleaned by hovering near leaves or tips of branches, aerially hawking, or hopping along stems and branches. This species' vocalizations consist of a series of thin, almost electronic-sounding buzzes, which variably ascend and descend in pitch.

MIGRATE? Mostly not.

NESTING: Selects a location adjacent to a junction of branches. The nest takes the shape of a rounded cup; it is woven with grasses and stems, and thickly bound with spider silk, which also anchors the nest to the tree. Not reused. About 2-3 in. wide.

EGGS: Off-white, with reddish-brown spotting. Length of ½ in. Total of 3-6, with 1-2 broods.

FEEDER BEHAVIOR: Does not visit feeders.

COMPARE TO SIMILAR SPECIES: The only other gnatcatcher to reside in North America is the Black-tailed Gnatcatcher, which is uncommon along the U.S.-Mexico border; the Black-tailed features a prominent black head cap.

DID YOU KNOW? The gnatcatchers are the sole North American representatives of the *Sylviidae* family, which primarily includes the Old World (or Eurasian) warblers. Intriguingly, this family is entirely genetically distinct from the *Parulidae* family of North American warblers.

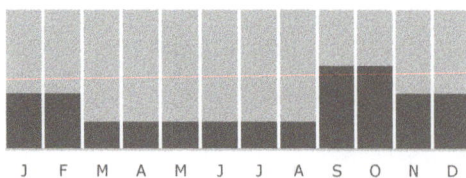

J F M A M J J A S O N D

Adults at top and bottom.

Adult at top (Photo by Andy Morffew / CC BY-SA / Cropped),
Adult at bottom.

② BROWN-HEADED NUTHATCH. *Sitta pusilla.*

SIZE: 4 in.

HABITAT: Southern pine forests, both open and dense.

WILD DIET: Insects and spiders, seeds and nuts.

BEHAVIOR: The smallest nuthatch of eastern North America, this species is often found hopping along tree trunks and branches in search of food. Insects are captured opportunistically in this manner; in winter, seeds and nuts are frequently lodged in the cranny or crevice of a tree, and hacked apart with the bill. Like other nuthatches, this species is also known to cache food under pieces of bark in the late fall and winter— providing a more reliable dietary source during the colder months. The calls of this Lilliputian species are remarkably akin to the sound of a rubber duck being squeezed.

MIGRATE? No.

NESTING: Cavity nester. Usually self-excavates, but may also use existing tree hollows or cavities. Inside, a bed of bark, grasses, and feathers lines the floor. About 4-5 in. across.

EGGS: White, with russet spotting. Length of ¾ in. Total of 3-8.

BIRD FEEDING TIPS

FEEDER DIET: Black-oil and hulled sunflower seeds, peanuts and peanut hearts, suet, mealworms. **FEEDER TYPES**: Tubes, hoppers, suet cages, platforms. **FEEDER BEHAVIOR**: Often observed making a series of quick visits, before flying away to hatch or store its haul. In winter, commonly associates with chickadees, woodpeckers, and pine warblers, among other seedeaters. Also, may use nest boxes.

COMPARE TO SIMILAR SPECIES: Compared to other nuthatches, this species' brown head and squeaky calls are most diagnostic.

DID YOU KNOW? Brown-headed Nuthatches are one of the few avian species which regularly demonstrates rudimentary tool use. In so doing, a strip of bark is peeled from a tree, and used to pry open crevices in search of hidden insects.

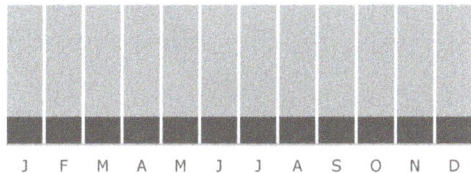

J F M A M J J A S O N D

① **RUBY-CROWNED KINGLET.** *Regulus calendula.*

SIZE: 4 in.

HABITAT: Breeds in mature, coniferous woods. During migration, often found in a variety of woods or thickets, including parks and suburbs.

WILD DIET: Insects (e.g., flies, ants) and spiders. Occasionally, fruits and seeds.

BEHAVIOR: This small bird has an enormously high metabolism, forcing it to forage actively all throughout the day. These caffeinated foraging habits often consist of hopping along branches, hovering near tips of branches or leaves, and sallying out into swarms of flying insects. Though less likely to flock with other kinglets during the breeding season—and often behaving quite territorially, with males flicking their rarely observed red head crests at rivals—this species often mixes with hordes of warblers and chickadees during migratory or wintering periods. Song is a distinctive mix of *seets*, chirps, trills, and slurs.

MIGRATE? Yes.

NESTING: Selects a location in a conifer. Nest is cup-shaped, and suspended from two or three branches, which are woven into the walls or rim of the nest. Constructed with a mix of grasses and feathers, and bound with spider silk. About 3-4 in. wide.

EGGS: Dull white. Length of ½ in. Total of 4-12.

FEEDER BEHAVIOR: Rarely visits feeders, usually for suet.

COMPARE TO SIMILAR SPECIES: Most similar to the closely related Golden-crowned Kinglet, which instead features a striped face and a visible golden-yellow head crest.

DID YOU KNOW? Relative to size, the kinglets lay the most eggs of any North American bird species. Just before laying, up to three-quarters of the female's weight may be comprised of her eggs alone—a truly remarkable feat.

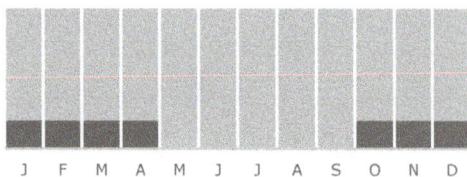

J F M A M J J A S O N D

Adults at top and bottom.

Adult male at top (Note: Red throat may appear blackish from a more severe angle),
Adult female at bottom.

③ **RUBY-THROATED HUMMINGBIRD.**
Archilochus colubris.

SIZE: 3 ¼ in.

HABITAT: Edges of woods, overgrown fields, gardens, suburbs.

WILD DIET: Nectar from flowers, flying insects. Also, sugar water from feeders.

BEHAVIOR: This high-revving species feeds on flower nectar all throughout the day, supplemented by a trickle of protein-rich, flying insects. Hovering and precise flight are facilitated by a wing mechanism unique to the hummingbird family: unlike other birds, which fold the wings on the upstroke, this species is able rotate its shoulders to provide propulsive thrust in all directions throughout a single wingbeat. Also like most hummingbirds, this species must feed every 15 minutes during the day to meet its exorbitant energy demands; during the nighttime, it compensates by entering a state of partial hibernation, known as *torpor*.

MIGRATE? Partially.

NESTING: Selects a location on top of a deciduous tree branch. Cup-shaped mound is formed of spider silk, pollen, and mosses. About 2 in. across.

EGGS: White. Length of ½ in. Total of 2. Raises 1-2 broods each year, occasionally 3.

BIRD FEEDING TIPS

FEEDER DIET: Sugar water. **FEEDER TYPES**: Nectar feeders. **FEEDER BEHAVIOR**: Perches or hovers at feeders. Males may act territorially near single-feeder setups.

COMPARE TO SIMILAR SPECIES: Males are quite distinctive across the region. Females of this species are very similar to female Black-chinned Hummingbirds, which normally summer in Texas and farther west; note that the female Ruby-throated's folded wingtips are straight and much slimmer.

DID YOU KNOW? Before migrating across the Gulf of Mexico, millions of hummingbirds gather along the coast, doubling their weights in the several days immediately preceding their departure. This ocean crossing is grueling, with up to one-quarter of all migrants failing to complete the perilous journey.

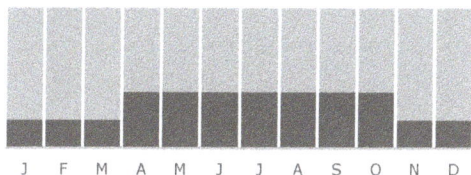

J F M A M J J A S O N D

299

INDEX OF SPECIES

SELECTED TITLES BY MARC PARNELL

The Birding Pro's Field Guides: City Series

Birds of Greater Chicago
Birds of Greater Cleveland, Pittsburgh, and Buffalo
Birds of Greater Dallas
Birds of Greater Houston
Birds of Greater New York City
Birds of Greater Washington, D.C.

The Birding Pro's Field Guides: State Series

Birds of Alabama
Birds of Arkansas
Birds of Connecticut
Birds of Delaware
Birds of Florida
Birds of Georgia
Birds of Iowa
Birds of Illinois
Birds of Indiana
Birds of Kansas
Birds of Kentucky
Birds of Louisiana
Birds of Massachusetts
Birds of Maryland
Birds of Michigan
Birds of Minnesota
Birds of Missouri

Birds of Mississippi
Birds of North Carolina
Birds of Nebraska
Birds of New Hampshire
Birds of New Jersey
Birds of New York
Birds of Ohio
Birds of Oklahoma
Birds of Pennsylvania
Birds of Rhode Island
Birds of South Carolina
Birds of Tennessee
Birds of Texas
Birds of Virginia
Birds of Vermont
Birds of Wisconsin
Birds of West Virginia

The Birding Pro's Field Guides: Province Series

Birds of Ontario

For a complete, updated list of titles, please visit our website at
www.thebirdingpro.com.

MARC PARNELL is a lifelong naturalist with a ceaseless passion for birding. He is currently the second most published ornithologist in the world by number of books in active print. Marc was born in Greenville, North Carolina, and presently resides in Cleveland, Ohio.

For press inquiries or event bookings, please contact the staff at Naturalist & Traveler Press, available at thebirdingpro.com.

If you enjoyed this field guide, please consider leaving a positive rating online at your place of purchase. As an independent publishing house, every bit of support is greatly appreciated.

Front Cover Photo: Swallow-tailed Kite
Back Cover Photos: American Kestrel, White-breasted Nuthatch

www.ingramcontent.com/pod-product-compliance
Lightning Source LLC
Chambersburg PA
CBHW040139270326
41928CB00022B/3258